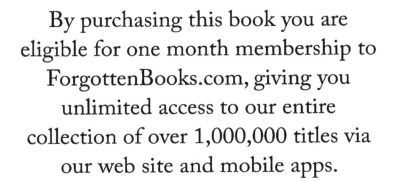

ISBN 978-0-331-41308-3
PIBN 11120384

LAND DEVELOPMENT PLAN

GREENVILLE, N.C.

DIVISION OF COMMUNITY PLANNING

The preparation of this report was financially aided through a
Federal grant from the Urban Renewal Administration of the
Department of Housing and Urban Development under the Urban
Planning Assistance Program authorized by Section 701 of the
Housing Act of 1954, as amended

THIS REPORT HAS BEEN PREPARED FOR
THE CITY OF GREENVILLE, NORTH CAROLINA

CITY COUNCIL

S. Eugene West, Mayor

Ralph F. W. Brimley

John L. Howard

Percy R. Cox

J.E. Clement

Harry E. Hagerty, City Manager

GREENVILLE CITY PLANNING AND ZONING COMMISSION
Kenneth G. Hite, Chairman

Frank L. Little   S. Eugene West, ex officio

Jerry Sutherland   Percy R. Cox, ex officio

H. T. Chapin, Jr.   Harry E. Hagerty, ex officio

Clarence B. Tugwell   Charles A. Holliday, ex officio

THIS REPORT HAS BEEN PREPARED BY
THE STATE OF NORTH CAROLINA
DEPARTMENT OF CONSERVATION AND DEVELOPMENT
DIVISION OF COMMUNITY PLANNING
George J. Monaghan, Administrator

COASTAL AREA OFFICE
James R. Hinkley, Director

PROJECT STAFF

William T. W. Kwan, Community Planner
Douglas L. Wiggins, Chief Draftsman
Marian J. Alligood, Secretary

January 1967   Price $1.00

FOREWORD

For nearly two decades, the City of Greenville has engaged in
various types of planning activities. In June 1947, the zoning
ordinance currently in use was adopted and by January 1954, a subdivision ordinance was incorporated into the City Code. Concerned
with the rapid urban growth in and around the community, the Municipal Administration, in early 1961, engaged the service of the
planning consultants, James B. Godwin & Associates of Raleigh,
N.C. to prepare a series of preliminary planning studies. These
documents, published over a period of two years, between July 1961
and September 1963, consist of the following:

Population and Economy Report, July 1961

Community Facilities Plan, September 1961

Public Improvements Program, January 1962

Land Use and Major Thoroughfare Plans, September 1963

In the meantime, other local programs related to planning were
underway within the community. Such activities include: Urban
Renewal, Public Housing, Building Code and Minimum Housing Code
Enforcement Programs, among others. During the same period, in
late 1963, the existing thoroughfare plan was adopted in its preliminary form by the municipality.

In April 1964, the Greenville City Council requested federal
assistance for financing further local planning activities. The
Division of Community Planning of the North Carolina Department
of Conservation and Development was contracted to provide technical
assistance for the preparation of the following planning elements:

Base Mapping

Land Use Survey and Analysis

Land Use Plan

Population and Economy Study

Neighborhood Analysis

Zoning Ordinance

Governmental Space Study

The first three elements listed above are included in this publication titled Land Development Plan of Greenville, N.C. The major land use objectives set forth in the Plan constitute the basis according to which the zoning ordinance currently in use will be revised. Although the adopted Thoroughfare Plan was formulated a scant three years before, several elements contained therein are already obsolete and prompt revisions are needed in accordance with the Land Development Plan. Among the various elements of this contract the Land Use Plan is, therefore, a pivotal study.

Of the other contractual elements, the Population and Economy Study has been published by the Division of Community Planning in 1965. A Governmental Space Study has been published in 1966, and a Neighborhood Analysis will be published in the latter part of 1966. The extensively revised Zoning Ordinance will be published upon its adoption by the local legislative body.

INTRODUCTION

The dormant eastern third of the State of North Carolina, a
geographically distinct region commonly known as East Carolina,
is reawakening and now standing on the threshold of a new cycle
of growth. This fast changing coastal plain region is currently
intensifying the search for a new identity and a new future. This
growing self-awareness in the region coincides with the timely
declaration of the community leaders of Greenville to become the
focal point of the East.

For Greenville, there are other aspirations as well. Indeed,
if and when such community wishes to come true, the city will
find itself at once a rejuvenated shopping magnet, a major industrial center, the same stronghold of tobacco warehousing, the
home of a superior region-wide medical health complex and, above
all, the education and culture center of the Coastal Plain Region.

These dreams do not materialize in the abstract, of course.
Their future fulfillment must take place within the physical confines of the urban space that is the present day Greenville and
its immediate environs. The communal aspirations must, therefore,
be expressed in concrete terms of land use: type, amount, location, functional relationship with other land uses, and others.

Certainly not to be ignored within the community are the
planning related problems, of which there are many and which
this study will reveal. A casual glance around would attest to
this assertion: the suburban sprawl, the vehicular congestion,
the visual disorder, and the extensiveness of neighborhood blight,
among other outstanding planning problems.

Hence, the major tasks that this study undertakes are four-
fold: First, to take stock of the existing land uses by major
categories and to project their respective quantity according to
the anticipated future needs of each; second, to identify,
analyze and offer corrective steps to the existing local planning
problems, the persistent presence of which may well pervert the
growth potential of the community; third, to translate the civic
aspirations into more clear-cut community goals and thence into

the realizable planning objectives; and finally, to accommodate the desired planning objectives by renovating the existing physical environs.

In no way should this study be regarded as a promotional brochure, for it is not its purpose to praise at a time and place when and where a proper diagnosis should be made. Nor should this study be construed as a "blue print" detailed for growth, for the information level provided by this study is never intended to penetrate beyond that of general guide lines. It is, however, the limited intention of this study to point out any basic conflicts and contradictions among the various civic aspirations, to relate the goals and objectives with respect to each other and to the natural setting and resources of the area, and, then, to suggest constructive steps to carry out such proposals.

The study is divided into three chapters. In Chapter I, the general background that provides the physical, social, and economic framework within which the community planning is to take place is presented. In Chapter II, the major categories of land uses within the community are analyzed, and the future space requirements of each are estimated. In the same chapter, various significant local planning problems are also given focus. In the last chapter, the various community goals are transformed into a coordinated plan of land uses and thoroughfares. In the closing sections of this chapter, the possible courses of action in implementing the various proposals of the plan are suggested.

Although the overall aim is to transform Greenville into a regional symbol of the coastal plain, the physical scope of the study is limited to the city proper and the immediate suburbs beyond. No regional plans or proposals are offered although a region-wide outlook is kept in mind throughout. A regional plan with Greenville as a focal center must await a future study.

MAP I
REGIONAL SETTING

CHAPTER I - PLANNING BACKGROUND

Section 1. Geographical and Historical Setting

Greenville, the county seat of Pitt County, is located in the north central portion of the coastal plain area that forms the eastern third of the State of North Carolina. Its precise geographical location* is given as 77° 20' 30" longitude and 35° 30' 20" latitude. Measured in distance as the crow flies, Greenville is about 72 miles nearly due east of Raleigh, the state capital; 120 miles southwest of Norfolk, Virginia, the largest metropolis as well as seaport among the vast coastal plain region that spans four states**; and an almost equal distance - 115 miles away from the Outer Banks at Cape Hatteras. Kinston, the nearest competing urban center of similar size, is situated about 28 miles to the south. Just a few miles to the east lies Beaufort County, the emerging mining and industrial center of the region. The alignments of the major north-south vehicular trunk line along the eastern seaboard - Interstate I-95 and U.S. 301 - are located to the west of Greenville and the county. Wilson, the nearest urban center along the routes, is approximately 30 aerial miles away.

Moved away from the now defunct urban place of Martinsborough in 1786, the then new county seat, Greenville was relocated at a new site which was central to all of Pitt County. The town was named after the Revolutionary War hero, General Nathaniel Greene of Guilford Courthouse fame, who died during the same year.

Greenville's 'first hundred acres' was located on the southern banks of the Tar River which is the major water course of the county region and was serving as the major, if not the only communication route of those early years.

---

*At Five Points in downtown Greenville.
**Virginia, North Carolina, South Carolina and Georgia.

The site of Greenville is characterized by the high,
generally well-drained southern banks where the major portion of
local urbanization has taken place. These higher southern banks
overlook a wide belt of almost impassible and periodically inundated swampy lowland which stretches nearly a mile in width in an
east-west direction. Green Mill Run, a major tributary of the
Tar River in the vicinity, flows northeastward through the city
and joins the main water course just to the east of Greenville.
The above described geographical peculiarity contributes significantly to the physical growth pattern of the city from its very
beginning to the present day.

The presence of the river with its adjacent stretch
of swampy lowland makes any early effort to urbanize the areas
north of the river an unprofitable and technically troublesome
venture. Land tracts suitable for urban development were simply
too distant to benefit from urban services at a time when commuting distance did not usually exceed one mile. Hence, before the
advent of the motor age, north Greenville was not locationally
suited for urbanization. Moreover, the high cost of bridging the
combination of the water course and its associated swampy lowland
further discouraged the urban development toward that direction.
Until very recently, only one road bridge linked the city proper
with its northern suburb.

Dictated by the geographical setting of its site,
Greenville has, therefore, from the very beginning, been restricted
in its physical growth to the south of the Tar River. As a result,
the community fanned out from the town center in the directions of
west, south and east until some other impediments to growth,
natural or manmade were reached.

In due time, the compact core of the original 'one
hundred acres' was further restricted in its future development
patterns by the imposition of other constraints to the growth of
the community. These physical constraints, described in the
following paragraphs, determined the present formation of the city
to a large degree.

The coming of the railroads and the establishment of the tobacco market warehousing have had definite effects on the physical growth pattern of Greenville. By the turn of this century several tobacco market auction warehouses already were situated on the then western edge of the city, along the tracks of the Atlantic Coast Line Railroad on both sides of Dickinson Avenue, then called the Plank Road. With the exception of limited residential development to the west of the railroad tracks between West Third and Fifth Streets, urbanization in the westerly direction was retarded until recent years.

Before the end of the first decade of the present century was reached another railroad came through Greenville and in a limited fashion, helped shape the southern boundary of the community for many years to come. The Norfolk Southern Railroad traversed the edge of the city from the south along an east-west axis at an average distance of about one mile south of the downtown thereby forming an artificial barrier to urbanization in that direction until after the end of World War II.

The single most important seed of growth for Greenville was planted in 1907. That was the year that the General Assembly authorized the establishment of East Carolina Teachers Training School. This educational institution, in search of a campus within the coastal plain region, found a home at the eastern edge of the community. About a hundred acres of rolling meadow land between East Fifth Street and Green Mill Run thus became the original site of the present East Carolina College.

A map dated 1903 shows the extent of urbanization in Greenville. It is interesting to note that east of present day Cotanche Street, there were no signs of urbanization. Although the placement of the college induced the residential growth to the north and southwest of the campus, the vastness of the college campus effectively delimited the eastern boundary of the city during the subsequent four and half decades.

During the ensuing decades the growth of the college at the eastern suburbs was counter balanced by the correspondent industrial, tobacco warehousing and wholesale growths centering

- 3 -

around the intersecting railroad axis and the major outward bound arterials notably Dickinson Avenue and South Evans Street. Without proper planning forethought, these industrial and warehousing establishments were allowed to be interspersed among several residential districts inhabited principally by low wage earners and their families. Unsound housing and poor neighborhood environment combined to erode considerable portions of the western suburb from within and without. Today, much of these older residential areas have degraded into a veritable slum - a civic burden that has only been recently felt by the entire community.

The days immediately after World War II marked the beginning of extensive suburbanization around Greenville. The pace of this explosive outward growth continues on unabated until today. Although the growth has expanded outward in every direction, the city has generally elongated along the north-south axis during the recent years. The college, meanwhile, had also expanded along the same axis. Further urban growth in the easterly direction necessarily means greater and more frequent penetration through the sprawling expanse of the ever enlarging campus. This explosive suburbanization, unchecked and unplanned, has now reached, in some places overreached, the limit of the community's natural drainage basin. Today, for its population size, Greenville ranks as one of the most physically extensive communities in the region: a dubious distinction that has definite ramifications in fiscal matters of the municipality.

Section 2. Social and Economic Profile*

    A. The Town Gown Symbiosis

While not detracting from the importance of other urban functions, the local phenomenon of town gown symbiosis has become increasingly the outstanding characteristic of Greenville during the recent years. The accompanying chart and graph (Tables 1 and 2) clearly indicate that the college is now, as it has been for the past two and one half decades, the major multiplier for

---

*Condensed largely from the study: Population and Economy of Greenville, Division of Community Planning, 1965.

TABLE 1 - POPULATION GROWTH - E.C.C. vs CITY OF GREENVILLE

| | College Related Population | | | Greenville City |
	Enrollment	Faculty & Empl.	Total	Population
1900	---	---	---	2,565
1910	142	40*	182*	4,101
1920	510	90*	600*	5,772
1930	923	120*	1,043*	9,194
1940	1,249	196	1,445	12,674
1950	1,891	259	2,150	16,724
1960	4,599	851	5,450	22,860
1965	6,599	961	7,560	28,533*

*Estimated

growth within the community, easily dominating the others such as manufacturing, construction, commerce, etc.

It is noted that whereas the noncollege related population in Greenville has been increasing linearly since 1920, gaining approximately 3,000 people during each succeeding decade, the college affiliated population, the sum total of student enrollment, faculty members and other college employees, has been gaining at an exponential rate, more than doubling in number each decade. The inflection point along the explosive growth curve apparently has not yet been reached. It should be pointed out that in both the table and the chart, the families of the faculty members and the college employees remain included under the noncollegiate population column thus tending to minimize the growth inpact of the college related population.

B. Population Projection

If the current trend continues for another decade, an entirely reasonable assumption, Greenville will have, by 1975, a noncollegiate population of between 23,000 and 25,000 persons, while the college related population will increase to between 14,000 and 16,000. Table 2 illustrates the past and the future population in Greenville. Estimates of 35,000, 41,000 and 45,000 are forecasted for the years 1970, 1975 and 1980 respectively, all high estimates. Since the noncollegiate population growth of the city during the recent years has been entirely due to repeated annexations of the built-up suburbs contiguous to the city limits, it is felt that the above future population projections for the 'city' may be used as the same projections for the planning area as well.

C. Current Population Estimate

The current population* estimate of Greenville is derived as follows: By using April 1960 noncollegiate population

---

*February 1966

TABLE 2
ENVILLE POPULATION– PAST TREND & FUTURE PROJECTION

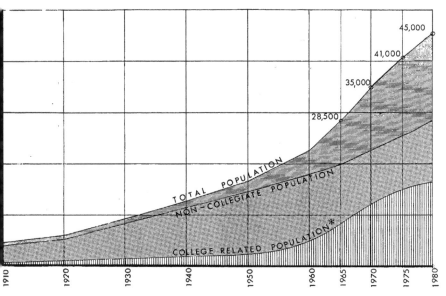

Including students, faculty members and other employees residing within city

as base, the following components are added thereto: population
gain by annexations, natural increase (births over deaths), net
migration, college students living on campus in February 1966
and college students living in Greenville, other than on campus,
in February 1966. This will provide a very reasonable estimate
of Greenville's total pdpulation as of the early part of 1966.
The derivation comes to 28,533 including the college students.

TABLE 3 - ESTIMATED CURRENT GREENVILLE POPULATION*

1.	Noncollegiate Population**, April, 1960	20,131
2.	Annexations Since That Date	3,080
3.	Natural Increase	1,750
4.	Migration (Net Loss).	-1,900
5.	E. C. C. Students Living on Campus.	3,933
6.	E. C. C. Students Living in City.	1,539
7.	Estimated Total Greenville Population	28,533

*February, 1966
**Including the Faculty Members and the College Employees

D. Other Population Characteristics

The nonwhite sector of the city's population growth
has not been keeping pace with that of the city as a whole. In
1930, the number of nonwhites in Greenville was slightly less
than half of the total population at 46.0%. Their relative
slackening pace of growth during the ensuing decades results in
a much smaller percentage today. The last census in 1960 shows
that 33.4% of the city's population are nonwhites. Undoubtedly,
this diminishing trend continues on and it is estimated that
currently only about 30.0% of the Greenville residents belong to
that category.

For the most part, almost all of the city's nonwhites
at present reside west of Evans Street. The greatest concentrations are found at the following areas: Cherry View, Ridgeway,
Biltmore, Lincoln Park, Riverdale, Higgs, South Pitt Street,
Kearney Park Public Housing Project and, far to the north of the
city, Edgemont and Greenfield Terrace.

- 7 -

The prevalent regional characteristics of outmigration of the local population are very much in evidence here in Greenville and especially in the county at large. Between 1950 and 1960, over 2,600 persons had outmigrated from within the city alone for a rate of 10.5%. For the county as a whole almost 10,000 persons had left for better opportunities elsewhere. The lack of employment opportunities within the immediate area has obviously affected the nonwhites considerably more than the rest. The outmigration ration between the two racial sections is more than three to one (3.8:1.0). Although the city's population has increased steadily, this was not accomplished at the expense of the county at large. Most of the newcomers inmigrating into Greenville have been the highly educated white-collar workers while the county continues to lose the unskilled and the unemployed blue-collar workers.

E. Education Characteristics*

The Town Gown symbiosis has its discordant aspects. The more obvious of these is the gap that exists between respective cultural standards of the various population sectors. Despite the presence of the large number of college related personnel, the overall level of educational attainment for adults in Greenville is in fact _lower_ than that of North Carolina's urban average - 9.9 versus 10.4 median school years completed.

The average educational attainment level of the non-whites is exactly one-half of that of the rest of the local population (6.1 years versus 12.2 years). More sobering, however, is the fact that the presence of each college graduate here in Greenville is more than matched by that of a functional illiterate.** While 16.6% of the whites receives 16 years of formal education or

---

*All figures are given by U.S. Bureau of Census, 1960.

**Legally defined as those who receive less than six years of formal education.

re, 23% of the same receives 6 years or less. Taking Greenville
a whole, 38% of the total adult population may be classified as
nctional illiterates. This discrepancy in educational levels
thin the city has significant implications in other socioecon-
ic aspects of community planning as well.*

F. Income Characteristics**
The latest information available related to local
comes dates no later than 1959. It is judged adequate neverthe-
ss for the purpose of this study which is to gain a relative
cture about its distribution pattern within the community.

Total personal income in Pitt County rose sharply dur-
g the past decade but not nearly as much as in most other North
rolina counties. In 1959, the county ranked 60th among the 100
unties in per capita income.

Estimates of county per capita income by the N.C.
partment of Tax Research for 1962 indicate that the level of
come has risen greatly since 1960. According to these estimates
tt County ranks 54th with a per capita income of $1,387 during
at year, which represents a significant increase in rank from a
sition of 60th only three years before.

But all these encouraging signs do not hide the fact
at a great concentration of poverty still exists within the
ty borders. Despite the various outward signs of affluence,
ose to 40% (38.5%) of all the families earned less than $3,000***
nually. Close to 2,000 families (1,957) received less than
,000 yearly and over 1,200 families earned less than $2,000. In
ew of this overwhelming prevalence of poverty, one can take little
mfort in noting that close to 500 families in the immediate vici-
ty belong to the $10,000 per year or up income group.

---

*See Neighborhood Analysis, Greenville, N.C.
**Population and Economy Study – Greenville, N.C.,
vision of Community Planning, Raleigh, 1964.
***The standard used in defining poverty.

The median income per family in Greenville was $3,915 per year, as compared with North Carolina urban average of $4,843 while the per capita income averaged out to be $1,123 per year as compared with the N.C. urban average of $1,639. Although both have increased since 1959, the exact distribution pattern at present is not known. Whether the large number of low income families has decreased or not remains to be surveyed by the coming 1970 federal census.

G. Employment Characteristics*

The detailed breakdown and the relative strengths of each sector of the employment group is given in Table 4. The index of specialization is a device whereby the relative strength of a given local employment sector is measured against that of the national average. Those above and below the norm of 1.00 are respectively over – and under specialized. Deviation from the national norm should not be construed as a sign of local economic distress. For instance, a college community such as Greenville should rightfully overspecialize in the "all education" category and underspecialize in heavy industries such as primary metals or machinery.

Taking the broad category of manufacturing as a whole, it is seen that Greenville falls short of being an industrial employment center as the index of 0.51 suggests. In reality, however, Greenville deserves a greater prominence than the statistics imply. All U.S. census data on employment groups is based on place of residence, but it is an established fact that a large number of the industrial workers in Eastern Carolina tend to commute, often across the county lines and beyond. In 1960, for example, 822 residents of other Counties reported to Census enumerators that they commuted to work in Pitt County. One thousand seven hundred fifty-one Pitt County residents reported that they commuted to work in other Counties.

---

*Population and Economy Study – Greenville, N.C.

Recent physical growth within the planning area is reflected in this table by the above average number of construction workers although this overspecialization is not an outstanding one.

Greenville's relatively poor location in the midst of the regional transportation network shows up in the subaverage index of specialization under the "transportation" column. The index would have been much lower were it not for the redeeming category of "communications." Although mainly belonging to the flow of information rather than goods, "communication" or "mass communication" is included under the transportation category. Due to the presence of the facilities of the Voice of America's broadcasting and transmission facilities as well as other mass media communication facilities, employment in communication shows outstanding strength in the community.

The relatively unimpressive index in commercial employment is misleading as the data are collected prior to 1960. In the outlying shopping centers several new commercial establishments, some of which are branches of the existing downtown retail establishments, are slated for openings during the latter half of 1966. Also, the relative unspecialized category of "business and repair service" needs a boost if Greenville is indeed to become an important white-collar employment center of the coastal region. There is apparently a large supply of domestics in the community as indicated by the specialization index which shows 50% above norm in the nation.

That Greenville is indeed a college community is given ample statistical support. In either total number being employed or in the index of specialization the "all education" category, already impressive in 1960, must have further increased since that date. The feeble showing among the other sectors of the "professional" groups of employment comes as a surprise. In medical health, public administration and other professional service groups where Greenville is expected to come to fore, the reverse is true. The materialization of the city as a future medical health center of the region would undoubtedly strengthen this particular employment sector.

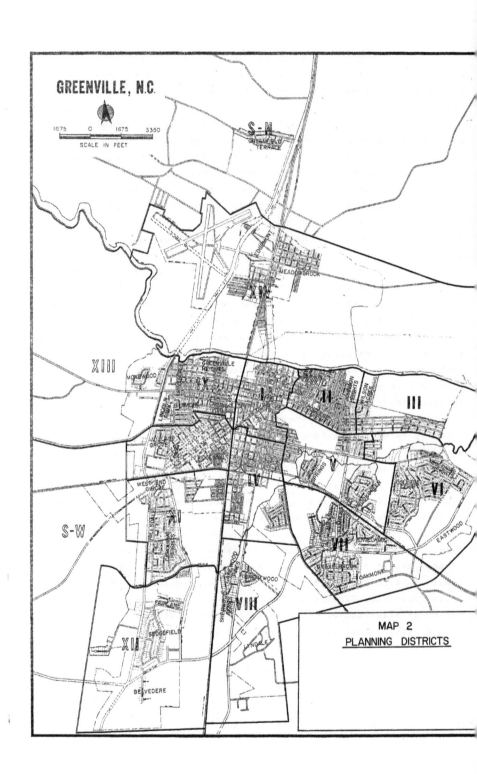

GREENVILLE, N.C.

1675   0   1675   3350
SCALE IN FEET

S-N
GREENFIELD
TERRACE

MAP 2
PLANNING DISTRICTS

CHAPTER II - LAND USE AND TRAFFIC ANALYSIS

Section 1. Planning Area, Planning Districts and General Land Use Statistics

The planning area delineated for this study is the same as that included by the city's extraterritorial zoning jurisdiction, extending one mile beyond the existing limits in all directions. For the purpose of convenient reference to a given location, the Greenville planning area is hereby conveniently subdivided into a mosaic of smaller areas called "planning districts." The total number of these districts is deliberately kept small - eighteen in all - including those in the outlying areas. In most instances, the size of each individual district is limited to no more than two or three local neighborhoods combined. With the exceptions of those containing the Central Business District and East Carolina College, each planning district is designed to accommodate ultimately between 2,500 and 3,000 people. The final delimitation of the districts' boundaries is determined by, insofar as may be allowed, the existing boundaries of "enumeration districts," the local area unit upon which the federal census information is based.

The locations and the boundaries of the planning districts are graphically shown in Map 2, while in Table 4, the equivalents of known local neighborhoods and enumeration districts are given for all planning districts.

Currently,* the City of Greenville extends 6.0 miles from Greenfield Terrace in the north to Belvedere in the south and 3.8 miles from Moyewood in the west to Eastwood at the eastern tip. Due to the highly irregularly shaped city limits, the area contained within the city is actually much smaller than the physical outlines suggest - about 5,850 acres or 9.1 square miles.** Of this acreage, close to 3,400 acres are currently developed for urban use, including those for thoroughfares, railroad rights-of-way, and the airport. Less than 60% of all land within the city, therefore, is currently urbanized.

---

*December of 1965.

**Figures furnished by the City Engineer's Office.

During late December of 1965, it was found that an
estimated population of 28,500 persons* were living in 7,296 dwelling units on approximately 1,365 acres of residential land. From
the above statistics, a local household size of 3.4 persons per
dwelling unit is derived. This figure is identical with that of
the urban North Carolina average. But the overall housing density
in Greenville is considered high - 5.3 dwellings per net acre or
about an average of 8,000 square feet per each residential lot.
The normal density for a growing neighborhood is about 4.0 dwelling units per net acre. Further detailed analyses on local residential land use in the planning area are presented in Section 2
of this Chapter.

In Table 5, the amount of land use by major categories
is given for selected periods during the recent past** while in
Map 3, the distribution pattern of the existing land uses are shown.
The land use statistics for the areas outside the municipality,
but within the planning area, are included under the "total" column.
The time dimension of the accompanying table provides a reasonably
reliable basis for estimating future land use requirements of various major categories within the Greenville Planning Area. In
projecting future land use requirements, only the planning area as
a whole is considered. It is felt that repeated future annexations
by the municipality would certainly upset the degree of accuracy of
any predictions of future land uses within the expanding city limits.
From the table, it is observed that in Greenville, vacant land is
being consumed for urban development purposes at a rate of approximately 135 acres each year. Between 40% and 50% of these newly
urbanized acres are for residential purposes. Correlating the
growth rate of various land use categories with that of anticipated
future population increases, about 720 acres, 1,430 acres, and
2,150 acres of additional land will be urbanized for 1970, 1975,
and 1980, respectively.

---

*Including students living on and off campus.

**The past land use information is extracted from Land
Use and Major Thoroughfare Plans, Greenville, N.C., Prepared by
J.B. Godwin and Associates, in 1963.

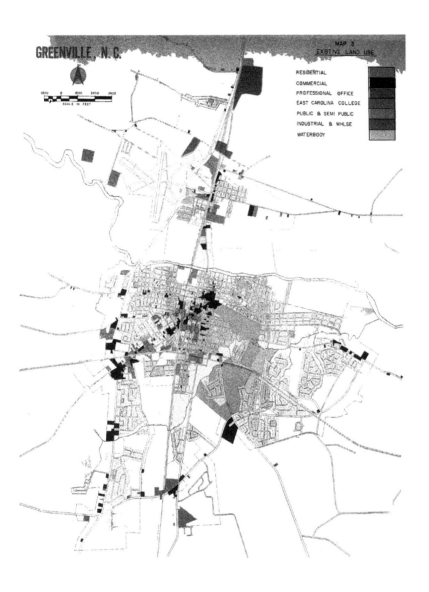

GREENVILLE, N.C.

SCALE IN FEET

MAP 3
EXISTING LAND USE

RESIDENTIAL
COMMERCIAL
PROFESSIONAL OFFICE
EAST CAROLINA COLLEGE
PUBLIC & SEMI PUBLIC
INDUSTRIAL & WHLSE
WATERBODY

TABLE 4 - PLANNING DISTRICTS

Planning District	Neighborhood Designation
I	Central Business - Shore Drive
II	College View - Johnson Heights
III	Wilson Acres - Green Springs, N.
IV	Evans Street South
V	Rock Springs - Brookgreen
VI	College Court - Eastwood
VII	Elmhurst - Drexelbrook
VIII	Lakewood Pines - Pitt Plaza
IX	Biltmore - Greenville Heights
X	Village Grove - Ridgeway
XI	Carolina Heights - South Greenville
XII	Fairlane - Belvedere
XIII	Memorial Hospital - Moyewood
XIV	Edgemont - Meadowbrook
S-N	Suburban North
S-W	Suburban West
S-S	Suburban South
S-E	Suburban East

GREENVILLE, N.C.

1675   0   1675   3360
SCALE IN FEET

MAP 4
HOUSING DENSITIES

AVERAGE LOT SIZE:

LESS THAN 4,500 SQ. FT.
4,500-8,000 SQ. FT.
8,000-15,000 SQ. FT.
OVER 15,000 SQ. FT.

Section 2. Residential Use of Land

Within the city limits, over forty percent of urban land is currently used for various residential purposes. This makes residential land use the largest among all land uses by far, as the second largest - public and semipublic use which includes the college, airport, parks, playgrounds and utility plants - consumes a much smaller 27.1% of all urban land. Of a total of 7,296 dwelling units* tabulated in late 1965 within the city, an overwhelming 75% belongs to the single, detached type. Slightly more than 1,200 dwelling units are housed in duplexes. The rest of the dwelling units are either in apartment or mobile home category, both of which total nearly 600 units.

Housing density and lot sizes are interrelated characteristics. It is generally true that in a typical urbanized area, smaller lot sizes denote greater housing density, with the exception of the still experimental cluster type of housing development in which each dwelling unit contributes a portion of its allotted land to a commonly owned open area. In Map 4, the pattern of housing density, according to the average lot size within a block, is graphically shown.

Referring to the same map, it may readily be seen that the older residential sections of the city tend invariably to have much smaller lot size; hence a higher housing density. In the residential neighborhoods to the north and southwest of East Carolina College, the individual lot size averages slightly above 5,000 square feet, whereas among the majority of newer middle income residential neighborhoods built since the end of World War II, the average size of the lot ranges between 8,000 to 12,000 square feet. Pockets of developments with extra large lots, 15,000 square feet or larger, dot the suburbs. Their presence serves to pinpoint the locations of the so-called exclusive neighborhoods in Greenville.

_____

*Including mobile homes and travel trailers used as permanent residences.

SCALE IN FEET

1675 0 1675 3350

MAP 5
HOUSING TYPES

DUPLEX
APARTMENT
MOBILE HOME PARK

Overly constrictive lot size, 4,500 square feet or
less, is synonymous with overcrowding and becomes a significant
contributor to housing blight. Their local presence, whether in
town or in the outlying districts, invariably coincides with other
symptoms of blight.* These slums or near slums may be readily
spotted and identified in Map 4; Shore Drive area in Planning
District I, the residential areas both sides of Norfolk-Southern
Railway west of South Evans Street in Planning District IV, the
Cherry View section of Planning District IX, and several others.

Map 5 is intended to show the distribution pattern of
various types of residential housing within the planning area.
Duplexes are concentrated primarily in the older neighborhoods
with higher housing density, the exception being the cluster of
new ones near the northern end of Elm Street in Planning District
II. South of the Norfolk-Southern Railway few, if any, duplexes
have been built, with the exception of a few along South Pitt
Street. It is safe to say that in Greenville, the duplex type of
housing is definitely associated with medium to high density residential neighborhoods.

The apartment type of housing in Greenville is found
in the following two locations: (1) higher density neighborhoods
immediately surrounding the College, where most of the smaller
apartments are located, and (2) along the major arterials in the
outlying areas where, during the most recent annexation, over
ninety apartments were taken in. Most of these units have been
constructed since 1960. Their rather sudden appearance along the
heavily traveled streets within the last few years tends to suggest a local multiplication of this type of housing.

A similar impression is gained by viewing the rapid
emergence of mobile homes within the planning area, either on
individual lots or grouped in mobile home parks. Unprecedented
local expansion in educational institutions and, to a certain extent, industrial facilities had precipated a long term housing

---

*See Neighborhood Analysis, Greenville, N.C.

shortage dating back to the late 1950's. Much simpler to finance than the apartments and without any regulatory standards to abide by, the mobile home parks of the "gypsy camp variety" have indeed spread all over the suburban landscape during the recent years.

With the exception of two relatively small concentrations in the Greenville Heights section of Planning District IX, there have been no sizable mobile home parks within the city limits until the recent annexation during which 74 mobile homes were taken in. Most of that number were grouped in three individual "parks." Single mobile homes, some of which are actually travel trailers, are found nevertheless throughout the older sections of the city on many individual lots.

Until the recent adoption of the new mobile home regulations, all of the mobile home parks found within the planning area were substandard in their exterior layouts as judged according to the recommended national standards. Almost invariably the allotted space for each mobile home stand measures not much more than 2,000 square feet. The environmental quality of the parks was so uniformly marginal that it took the unusually high average educational and social backgrounds of the occupants to save these mobile home parks from becoming high density rural slums. The recently enacted Mobile Home Regulations were adopted in the fervent hope that such substandard neighborhoods will not recur within the planning area.

As a significant step in the elimination of local housing blight, several sizable low rent housing projects have been initiated during the recent years and one project has been completed. Over four hundred publicly owned and maintained dwellings are to replace a significant portion of the substandard homes found in various concentrations throughout the older declining neighborhoods of the city. Two such projects, totaling more than 250 units, are currently in search of suitable sites. For a more detailed discussion of various aspects of public housing in Greenville, the study titled "Neighborhood Analysis, Greenville, N.C." should be consulted.

Section 3. Retail Service and Trades, Office and Professional
Use of Land

As previously tabulated in Table 5, land utilized for
various types of commercial uses is estimated at 230.8 acres. Of
this acreage, only 7.2% or 16.6 acres, are located within the
traditional downtown area - the compact mercantile district bounded
by, in clockwise fashion: First, Reade, Eighth, Dickinson and
Greene Streets. The balance of the commercial acreage is distributed throughout the various parts of the city in the following
manner: (a) local neighborhood business centers, (b) regionally
oriented shopping centers, and (c) commercial strips along major
traffic arterials within the planning area.

In terms of the number of business establishments,
downtown Greenville remains to be the dominant center within the
planning area. Despite the steady increase of competition from
the outlying commercial strips and centers, the downtown, with
less than 10% of total commercial land, contains 56% of the establishments. This greater density of business firms indicates the
following: that downtown Greenville offers greater variety of
shopping choices; and that, within the downtown area the high
percentage of land occupied by the buildings denotes a correspond-
ing lack of available parking spaces. Indeed, off-street parking
provided by individual business firms, for either visiting public
or employees, is at a bare minimum in downtown Greenville.

The often heard contention that downtown's main attri-
bute is its conduciveness for face-to-face contacts is quite
dramatically born out by the statistics revealed in Table 6. Although the concentration of retail and convenience service trades
within this traditional core area is considerable, the marked
gravitation of white-collar professionals into the downtown precinct is overwhelming. By actual count, over three quarters of
these professionals currently attend to their clients in a roughly
circular zone immediately surrounding the downtown retail core.
Some decentralization of the office and institutional activities
has occurred during the recent years. Dilapidation of physical
quarters, lack of opportunity to expand, severe shortage of off-

- 18 -

street parking, among others, were given as the cause to relocate.*
Evans Street, immediately to the south of the Central Business
District, appears to have caught the bulk of the fallout. Two
other minor concentrations of the white-collar professionals exist
within the planning area, one being the so-called "old hospital
building" north of the college in Planning District II, and the
other being the new hospital complex at the western edge of the
city in Planning District XIII.

The analysis and proposals related to the "old hospital building" have been given elsewhere* and are not repeated here.
The new hospital complex appears to possess good potential in
expanding into a regionwide medical health complex; more of the
same topic will be further discussed in the following sections.

Aside from the usual members of the typical neighborhood stores – the corner drugstores, family groceries, laundromats
and so forth, which are found in small numbers in the midst of
many residential neighborhoods, several large scale shopping centers have appeared on the local scene. All of these centers are
located in the outlying areas at the intersections of major
arterials and circumferential highways. The preconditions in the
establishment of these shopping centers consist of the following:
large tract of land for the ready accommodation of ample parking
and the expansion of the one storied commercial structure, relative cheap price of land, and the easy accessibility for the
predominantly automobile oriented shoppers.

The first of the three centers currently in operation
is also the smallest. Situated near the intersection of Fifth and
Tenth Streets, College View Shopping Center occupies only one and
one-half acres and contains approximately 16 establishments. It is
also the only shopping center in Greenville with no major retail

---

*Refer to <u>Governmental Space Study, Greenville, N.C.</u>,
published in June 1966, for more detailed information on local
public office space demands.

TABLE 5

EXISTING LAND USE STATISTICS AND FUTURE ESTIMATES

| | Existing Land Uses | | | | | | | | | | | | Projected Planning Land Use Acreage | | |
| | 1961 Acreage | | | | 1963 Acreage | | | | 1965 Acreage | | | | | | |
	City	Percent	Planning Area	Percent	City	Percent	Planning Area	Percent	City	Percent	Planning Area	Percent	1970	1975	1980
Residential	1077.3	38.1	1438.4	48.0	1177.3	39.7	1557.9	49.6	1382.2	41.2	1802.2	39.3	2360.0	2910.0	3450.0
Commercial	121.6	4.3	190.6	6.4	153.4	7.8	210.6	6.7	213.6	6.2	230.8	5.0	255.0	280.0	305.0
Wholesale General	81.6	2.9	94.5	3.1	81.6	2.7	94.5	3.0	38.8	1.1	96.1	2.2	98.0	100.0	102.0
Tobacco	36.6	1.3	63.2	2.1	36.6	1.2	63.4	2.0	46.9	1.3	63.2	1.4	65.0	68.5	72.0
Industrial	87.3	3.1	118.8	4.0	87.3	2.9	134.4	4.3	143.9	4.1	274.9	6.0	374.0	454.0	514.0
Public & Semi-Public	720.4	25.6	1028.0	34.3	723.5	24.3	990.8	31.6	910.1	27.1	1038.0	22.7	1060.0	1095.0	1130.0
Transportation (except streets)	30.1	1.1	76.9	2.5	32.3	1.1	77.2	2.5	34.1	1.0	78.7	1.6	79.0	81.0	83.0
Streets	664.7	23.6	987.3	32.9	674.6	27.4	996.7	31.8	769.2	23.0	1006.5	21.8	1018.0	1035.5	1050.0
Total Urban	2819.6	100.0	3010.4	100.0	2966.5	100.0	3128.2	100.0	3346.3	100.0	4591.4	100.0	5308.0	6023.0	6706.0
Total Urban	2819.6	65.1	3010.4	21.2	2966.5	62.2	3128.2	22.1	3346.3	57.5	4591.4	30.4	---	---	---
Vacant Land	1505.0	34.9	10140.4	78.8	1806.2	37.8	10007.3	77.9	2503.5	42.5	10506.6	69.6	---	---	---
Gross Area	4324.6	100.0	14138.1	100.0	4772.7	100.0	14138.1	100.0	5850.0	100.0	15098.0	100.0	---	---	---

magnet. The center at West End Circle at the intersection of Dickinson Avenue and N.C. Highway 11 came into being less than two years ago and has two major retail magnets. The existing acreage of 7.9 can be eventually expanded to about 16 acres. The latest and the biggest of the trio is the Pitt Plaza located at the intersection of New Bern Highway (N.C. 43) and Greenville Boulevard (U.S. 264 Bypass) and situated on approximately 21 acres of land.

TABLE 6 - DISTRIBUTION OF COMMERCIAL ACTIVITIES

Number of Establishments, 1965

	Downtown	City Total	% of Total that are Downtown
Retail	81	186	44
Service	77	201	39
Professional and Institutional	203	260	77
Total	361	647	56

This shopping center, with four or possibly five major national chain stores together with more than two dozen supporting convenience trade facilities, unquestionably will pose the strongest challenge to downtown Greenville within a radius of 35 miles. The gross leasable floor area with approximately 180,000 square feet is about 30% of that of downtown. With an average sales figure of $50 per square foot of floor space,* it may be safe to conclude that these shopping centers, when fully developed, will seriously erode the downtown shopping potential. They will, however, make Greenville more competitive as a retail center in Eastern North Carolina and provide employment for a large number of store managers, clerks, etc.

---

*See The Dollars and Cents of Shopping Centers - 1960, Urban Land Institute.

Another seemingly inevitable byproduct of contemporary
urban growth is the development of strip commercial establishments
along the major highways at the urban fringe. This has been very
much in evidence in Greenville. With the continuing rise in local
motor vehicle registration and a steady increase in intercity
travel, the growth of such commercial activities will not be intensified. The analysis which follows is intended to show that
if the above related development is allowed to continue unchecked,
this type of activity would be developed at the expense of the
local public safety and welfare and become self-defeating in the
end.

Within the Greenville planning area, the aphid-like
commercial growths along the stalks of highways occur principally
along South Dickinson Avenue and Memorial Drive (N.C. 11), North
Greene Street between the River and the Pactolus Highway, the
southern portion of Greenville Boulevard (U.S. 264 Bypass), the
eastern third of Tenth Street and the entire length of Dickinson
Avenue from West End Circle to downtown. Dickinson Avenue, North
Greene Street and East Tenth Street are urban arterials while the
other two are classified as circumferential loop roads.

The prime purpose of any thoroughfare is to expedite
the flow of traffic and provide access for the motoring public.
If these arterials and loop roads fail in this capacity, then they
defeat their purpose, with the result that the bypasses themselves
will soon be bypassed.

A noted authority* in traffic engineering researching
on the same subject has been able to reach the following conclu-
sions:

- The delay and congestion resulting from commercial
  roadside development are very substantial in terms
  of loss of time, confort and convenience.

- The delay so caused can be attributed to a combination of two factors: (a) physical factors and (b)
  psychological factors.

---

*Professor W. Horn in "The Effects of Commercial Road-
side Development on Traffic Operations," N.C. State University,
publication, 1960.

- Psychological factors are found to be the major cause
  and they can be eliminated only through the physical
  removal of the conflict-causing commercial developments.

- The increased road uses costs thus resulted amply
  justify that extensive planning and improvements be
  made for any section of highway that already has
  been or is expected to be heavily commercialized.

Along South Dickinson Avenue between West End Circle
and U.S. 264 Bypass, a total of 112 curb-cuts or driveway connections were counted representing 29 commercial establishments
(with 57 driveway connections) and 55 residential structures.

Along Greenville Boulevard (264 Bypass) between South
Dickinson Avenue and the New Bern Highway, 43 driveway connections
representing 21 commercial establishments and 12 residential structures were tabulated. The land along these two thoroughfares is
showing signs of being rapidly commercialized or otherwise developed.
No regulatory measure, however, is currently available to guide the
desirable growth or to prevent the further erosion of the existing
service level of these thoroughfares. Some prompt regulatory measures to control the strip commercial development along the major
arterials in Greenville are needed.

Section 4. Industrial and Wholesale Use of Land

Land use activities to be discussed in this section
consist of three broad categories: manufacturing, service type
industry, and wholesaling activities which are predominantly
tobacco warehousing.

With few exceptions, industrial use of land within
the Greenville planning area follows rather predictable patterns.
South of the Tar River, there is no industrial land use east of
Cotanche Street, and with the exception of Union Carbide, all
other industrial uses are confined to the immediate vicinities of
the two railroads - Norfolk Southern and Atlantic Coast Lines -
and at the intersections of the railroads and major thoroughfares,
mainly Dickinson Avenue, Tenth Street and Memorial Drive North
(N.C. 11).

- 23 -

Within the older urbanized area, industrial land uses
are concentrated in and around a triangular zone shaped by the
two railroads, with their spur lines and Dickinson Avenue. In
the outlying areas where all but one (Fieldcrest Mills), major
manufacturing plants are located, industrial uses of land prefer
the close association of major thoroughfare and railroad. The
river, once a major transportation channel, now plays no part in
the local industrial scene, save to serve as the source of water
intake for the Utility Commission's water plant.

Without exception, industrial plants and warehouses
in the older sections of the urbanized area, are located in obsolete physical plants on very small lots. Off-street parking and
loading facilities are woefully inadequate by modern standards.
Lack of building setbacks often becomes a source of traffic problems at the street intersections due to the poor line of sight -
a safety feature so heavily stressed in residential subdivision
standards. Efficiency in the use of this in-town industrial land
is limited by the odd shape of the land parcel prevalent in the
triangular zone. Moreover, the noise, odor, vibration and other
nuisances of these industrial developments create an unhealthy
environment for the significant number of residential pockets
nested among the plants and warehouses. It has been shown* in a
parallel study that mixing industrial and residential land use
often contributes to blight and the gradual but certain decline
of the inner core of the community.

Industrial uses in the outlying districts are invariably accorded much larger tracts of land - 15 acres or more. Here
the overcrowding that plagues in-town industrial plants is absent
and off-street parking and loading provisions are quite satis-
factory.

---

*See Neighborhood Analysis, Greenville, N.C., pub-
lished December 1966, with this study by the Division of Community Planning.

The commonly accepted rule of thumb of 10 employees per acre comes close to being met for these outlying industrial plants. Assuming that the pace of automation does not suddenly quicken, the above ratio may be used for setting minimum lot requirements for all future industrial land uses in the greater Greenville area.

Operating five sets of buyers simultaneously when in season, Greenville is one of the largest two or three tobacco warehousing centers in the Eastern Belt. Currently, there are twenty tobacco warehouses and nine warehouse firms in Greenville with more than three _million_ square feet of floor space devoted to the sale and processing of leaf tobacco. While most of these warehouses are located in the triangular zone in town, the newest and the largest - over six acres of floor space - is located north of the Tar River on 22 acres of land. The emerging trend in locating new tobacco warehousing appears to be that of the above described, in the outlying suburb, with ample acreage along major highways. It is entirely reasonable to exclude in the future this particular use that is inactive for over forty weeks of a year from a highly urbanized core of the city.

Section 5. Public and Semipublic Use of Land

Publicly owned and/or public oriented land uses such as hospital, cemeteries, parks, playgrounds, schools, garbage dumps and other similar facilities are included in this category. East Carolina College, because of its size and importance, is discussed separately in the following section. Within the scope consigned to this study, the analysis addresses itself strictly to the land use aspects of the facilities included - the distribution pattern, the total and individual acreage and the functional relationship with other land uses within the planning area. Topics that touch upon the discussion of the quality and the quantity of the various facilities must await further detailed studies, such as a Community Facilities Study.

The usable recreational land open to the public totals approximately 62 acres, all of which except 0.70 acres in Meadowbrook off Munford Road in Planning District XIV are owned by the

municipality. Table 7 presents a locational and acreage breakdown of the recreation land within the city. It should be added
that currently the city does not own land for recreational purposes beyond the city limits.

TABLE 7 - LOCATION AND SIZE OF RECREATION LAND

NAME	LOCATION	
Elm Street Park	Elm Street	4.77
Greenfield Terrace	Greenfield Boulevard	2.06
Greensprings Park	East Fifth Street	25.56
Guy Smith Stadium	Chestnut Street	12.17
Hillsdale Park	Sunset Avenue	0.72
Kiwanis Train	Elm Street	3.64
Peppermint Park	Brownlee Drive and 14th	1.14
Shore Drive Park	Shore Drive	1.64
South Greenville	Howell Street	9.09
South Wright Road	South Wright Road	0.20
Woodlawn Park	Park Dr. & Woodlawn Avenue	0.63
Subtotal		61.62
Meadowbrook*	Mumford Road	0.70

*Leased open area

        In terms of acreage, the total amount of recreational
land in Greenville is short of the regional standard of one acre
of open land per each one hundred (100) population. For a pro-
jected noncollegiate population* of 24,000 in 1970, 240 acres of
recreation land, not all of which would have to be within the city,
are needed to serve the community. Even allowing the fact that
the college campus may be partially subsituated for the needed recreation land, the four to one ratio that exists between what is
existing and what is needed indicates a significant deficit in
local recreation land.
        A faulty distribution pattern of the recreational
land is also observed. The locational criteria decree that such
land should be centrally located with respect to its potential users.

_____

*See Section 2, Chapter 1 of this study.

A comparison between their present locations and the existing population densities, i.e. housing densities shown in Map 4, readily reveals the discrepancies. In Greenville, higher population density prevails in three general neighborhoods: Planning District II, north of the College; Planning District IX, in Cherry View and Greenville Height section; and Planning District X in the Ridgeway section. Within these areas a mere 12.8 acres are counted, the bulk of which (12.2 acres) belongs to Guy Smith Stadium in Planning District X. In Planning District II, only small Woodlawn Park with 0.6 acres serves the whole neighborhood between the college and the river. There is no park of any description that serves Planning District IX, the Greenville Heights-Cherry View section. Within these areas, school grounds and most likely the streets provide the only areas where the young ones can play.

The emerging residential neighborhoods in the southern part of the city are also showing a total lack of recreation land. In Planning District XII, from Fairlane to Belvedere in Planning District VII, from Lake Wood Pines to Pitt Plaza in Planning District VII Elmhurst-Drexelbrook, there is no usable open land reserved for neighborhood recreational purposes. Unless positive steps are soon taken, costly remedial actions may have to be the answer in the future because these areas are rapidly being urbanized.

The three municipal facilities - cemetery, sewage disposal plant and city dump - are located in close proximity to each other near the confluence of the Tar River and Green Mill Run at the eastern edge of the city. The steady eastward advance of urbanization and the climatical factor of the local prevailing wind* may, in the near future, make the city dump a nuisance. Suitably located acreage further out in the suburbs will have to be acquired in order to accommodate the sanitary disposal of the refuse.

The Pitt Memorial Hospital with 206 beds, located on 29½ acres of land on the western edge of the city off the Falkland

---

*From the northeast in fall and from the southwest during the rest of the year.

Highway, serves the county region at large. The accessibility by
the visiting public from the northwest to the southwest quadrant
of the county appears to be quite adequate whereas from the northeast and southeast, persons enroute to the hospital may be unduly
delayed by the poor street network in and around the city.

Section 6. East Carolina College

The growth of East Carolina College originally started
in the then eastern suburb of Greenville shortly after the turn of
the current century. Located along the southside of Fifth Street,
the campus has, through the years, expanded clockwise eastward and
southward. Today, the College, with its immense area of 298 acres,
is split among five radiating urban thoroughfares: Fifth, Tenth,
Fourteenth, Charles and Evans Streets and finds itself situated
very much near the center of the city.

The land use pattern within the campus is as follows:
The administrative center, the library, the classrooms and the
women's dormitories are located in the older part of the campus -
between Fifth and Tenth Streets; mens' dormitories are situated
in the middle campus between Tenth and Fourteenth Streets; all
athletic activities, including Ficklen Stadium, are located south
of the railroads with the major entrance from Charles Street or
N.C. 43; all other college owned lands west of Charles Street are
currently held as future land reserve.

As of the fall of 1965, the total enrollment of the
East Carolina College was 7,728. A further breakdown shows that
there were 3,933 students living in dormitories, 389 in fraternity
or sorority homes, 1,150 living off campus in Greenville and 2,256
commuting from elsewhere. The total enrollment declined somewhat
to 7,510 during the spring semester. The number of registered
motor vehicles, excluding motorcycles and scooters, however, shows
a phenomenal increase from 3,724 during the fall to 5,034 counted
in March of 1966.

The observed intracampus movement is overwhelmingly
pedestrian along a north-south axis for the male students and east-
west axis for the women students. There is an increasing amount of

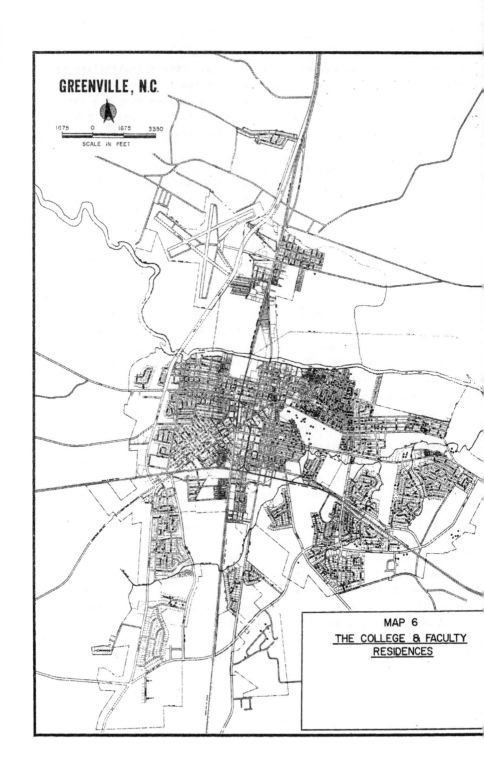

GREENVILLE, N.C.

1675   0   1675   3350
SCALE IN FEET

MAP 6
THE COLLEGE & FACULTY
RESIDENCES

street crossing by the students on foot between the various parts
of the campus. It should be noted that all of the urban streets
that separate the campus are major thoroughfares. The anticipated
increase of vehicular traffic along these thoroughfares, therefore,
stands in direct conflict with the future increase of student enrollment which would undoubtedly create an even more intensified
pedestrian movement across the campus. There is no compilation
of where the in-town day students reside, but a survey does graphically indicate in Map 6 where the faculty members are located. If
it is assumed that the day students more or less follow the similar locational characteristics, then there is much pedestrian
crossing on Fifth as well as on Fourth Streets.

Parking problems, on campus as well as off campus, have
become more acute during the recent years. Despite stringent regulations and policies decreed by the college authorities, the
general situation has worsened. A ban of parking on campus merely
means a proportional spillover to the neighboring residential
streets. The anticipated increase of enrollment to a peak of some
12,000 students by about 1980 would certainly create a situation,
in parking as well as in general traffic patterns, in and around
the campus which may soon be untenable, if the present arrangements
are allowed to persist.

Although the major planning problems created by the
presence of the college are traffic and parking, certain aspects
of future land use anticipated by the College also warrant some
serious consideration. Amidst much talk about the impending
arrival of a medical school in Greenville under the auspices of
the East Carolina College, location of the facility has not been
carefully considered. There have been vague suggestions about
utilizing the open land currently owned by the College west of
Charles Street, although the majority of the four year medical
schools throughout this country are physically as well as functionally linked to a hospital. If the construction of another
hospital is not anticipated within this community, the proper
location for the proposed medical school should logically be
placed in the vicinity off Falkland Highway and Memorial Drive

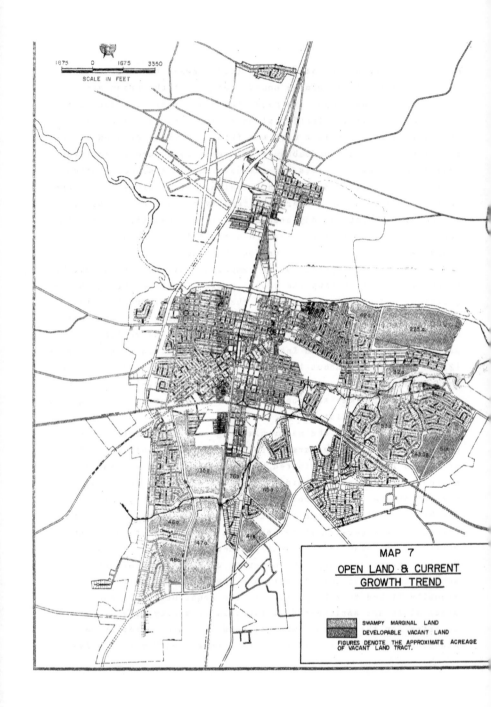

SCALE IN FEET

1675   0   1675   3350

MAP 7

OPEN LAND & CURRENT
GROWTH TREND

SWAMPY MARGINAL LAND
DEVELOPABLE VACANT LAND
FIGURES DENOTE THE APPROXIMATE ACREAGE
OF VACANT LAND TRACT.

where the functionally related medical facilities are currently
situated, providing, of course, that land parcels of proper acreage are available.

Section 7. Open Land and Recent Development Trends

The phenomenon of the local urban sprawl is closely
related to the distribution pattern of the open land which may be
one of the following: farmland, currently in use or discontinued;
woodland, swampy or otherwise. A typical pattern of suburbanization in Greenville during the recent years has been the growth of
an outlying residential neighborhood leapfrogging considerable
expanse of open space. Together with the sprawling college campus,
this vast acreage of nonurban land provides an internal padding
of the physical community and makes Greenville appear much larger.

Although large acreage of nonurban land in the midst
of the densely developed area is not uncommon to many growing communities, the extremeness of this phenomena here in Greenville
deserves further attention. In Map 7, among other information,
the general location and extent of these tracts of land currently
existing within the planning area is shown.

Not all of these vacant tracts are readily developable.
The presence of wooded swamp land just to the north of Tar River,
for instance, effectively prevents any form of higher urban development within a broad belt of nearly one mile. Beyond that distance, the airport further deters any attempt of urbanization in
the northwesterly direction. These two factors are mainly responsible for the retardation in the urban development in the north
Greenville area.

South of the river, with the exception of the wooded
lowland along Green Mill Run and parts of its tributaries, all of
the currently undeveloped tracts may be readily converted to urban
use. Within the area bounded by the River in the north, N.C. 11
in the west, U.S. 264 Bypass to the south and east, nine such
tracts of land are counted totaling some 1,070 acres*.

---

*Not including the wooded swampy land along the Green
Mill Run and its tributaries.

One reason for excessive sprawl may be due to the co-existence of town and country, or the value of the farmland currently in use, versus that of the improved land for urban development. Unlike urban centers in other regions, Greenville is situated deep in the heart of a tobacco rich agricultural region. The high price of farmland, especially that with tobacco allotment, constantly competes with the cost of urban improvements. Much of the open land in the community is cropland as Map 7 indicates.

Although the exact acreage of tobacco allotment within these tracts of open cropland is not known, that there is a considerable amount of such use is nevertheless quite certain. At approximately $5,000 per acre of tobacco allotment, this so-called nonurban land apparently may offer stiff competition to local urbanization for some years to come.

Map 7 also shows the local building permits issued during the past 30 months.* Since the vast majority of permits issued in this area are for new residential construction, the trends in local development can easily be seen. The community continues to expand, residentially as well as commercially, in the general directions of south and east. New population growth in the outlying areas is accentuated by recent construction of apartment complexes. The traditional open land remains bypassed and forsaken by the developers for the greener pastures even further beyond.

Section 8. Traffic Analysis

The crux of Greenville's planning problems lies in the malfunctioning of its street system. It cannot be denied that the presence of geographical barriers compounded by a lack of coordination among various local sectors of growth adds much to the present woes of the municipality. But it is also evident that a sound policy has never been formulated.

---

*From January of 1964 through May 1966.

The thoroughfare plan currently in use is divorced
from local realities to an alarming extent. It appears to consist of a combination of existing make-dos and wholly impractical
future proposals. It is neither capable of solving present exigencies nor designed to help in carrying out the desired communal
objectives. In fact, should the contents of the plan be implemented, the overall traffic situation in Greenville would actually
be worsened. Presented in detail below are a series of critiques
concerning the traffic conditions currently existing in the community. Analyses are to be given on three levels: the system,
the specifics and the general policy.

I. The System. The layout of Greenville's traffic
system is imperfectly constructed. With few exceptions the con-
verging arterials and the bypassing inner or outer loops are
physically obstructed after only relatively short runs and such
interruptions often occur at crucial locations. At present, there
is not a single complete loop street or through arterial worthy
of its functional description in existence within the local traffic system. The longest run of all the thoroughfares is the N.C.
11 Bypass, although along this route, a severe "kink" exists at
West End Circle. Fifth Street, laid out along the east-west axis,
has a similar jog obstruction at the intersection of Albemarle
Street. Also the through pattern of Fifth Street is effectively
disrupted at Green Street intersection where the downtown one-way
street pattern becomes effective.

Although theoretically N.C. 11 (Memorial Drive and
South Dickinson) and U.S. 264 Bypass (Greenville Boulevard) should
form an interconnected three quarter loop, in reality due to the
unusual alignment of the 264 Bypass, such a loop is not functional
since it would take the motorist far to the south near Belvedere
before orienting northward again. A resident of Eastwood might as
well brace the urban congestion in order to reach the airport,
fairground, or the growing industrial areas beyond. A student
residing in a mobile home park near Green Springs Park must travel
some five and a half miles or nearly ten minutes of travel time
in order to reach the mobile home of another located in the new

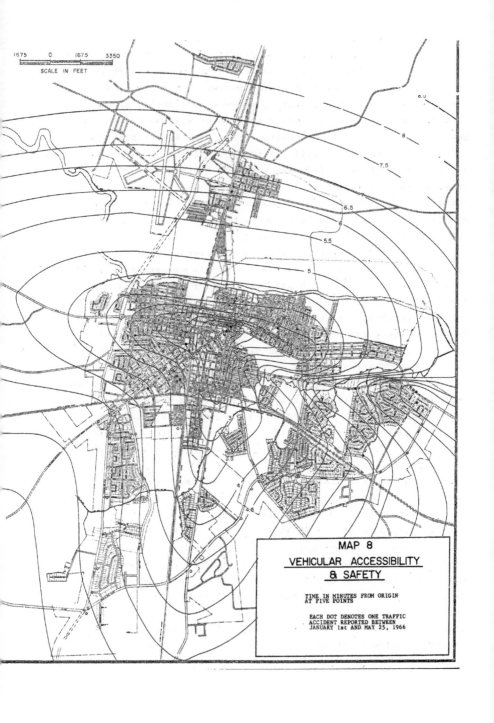

SCALE IN FEET

1675   0   1675   3350

MAP 8

VEHICULAR ACCESSIBILITY
& SAFETY

TIME IN MINUTES FROM ORIGIN
AT FIVE POINTS

EACH DOT DENOTES ONE TRAFFIC
ACCIDENT REPORTED BETWEEN
JANUARY 1st AND MAY 25, 1966

park at the eastern end of Mumford Road, although the straight
line distance between the two is less than one and half miles.
Similar inconvenience may be cited for the shoppers who might
wish to do some comparison shopping between the two emerging shopping centers - Pitt Plaza and West End Circle; or the not unlikely
case of a physician attending a game in Ficklen Stadium whose presence is suddenly needed in the Pitt Memorial Hospital. The common occurrence of such inconveniences should not be in itself
surprising. What is amazing is that for so long no constructive
action has yet been undertaken to amend the situation.

The present layout of the thoroughfare network heavily
favors the convergence of the arterials such as Dickinson Avenue,
Evans, Charles and Fifth Street toward downtown Greenville. The
basic reasons behind the concept which decrees that all roads lead
to downtown, however, have long since disappeared. In the horse
and buggy days of yore, Five Points was indeed the hub of the
region. Save for the geographical intervention of the River, even
more points would have converged.

Today, the centers of various community activities no
longer concentrate all in that one locale - downtown. In Greenville, there is a "fallout" of such activity centers: the satellite
commercial centers, the college related instruction and athletic
centers, medical centers and industrial centers. The sharing of
the stage with downtown Greenville gives these decentralized outlying centers an importance that should be properly reflected in
the design of a revised transportation network. The street network
of tomorrow for Greenville will probably be more grid like because
of the counterbalance created by the several major activity centers
that will be greatly developed within the community.

The presence of a major street in a neighborhood may
be taken as a resulting sign of urban development. More often
though, it is a sure indication that new development is about to
take place. In other words, the construction or even the alignment of a major thoroughfare is a very important tool for promoting
urban growth. It thus follows that the future physical growth
pattern of a community depends to a considerable extent upon the
proposed alignment of the thoroughfare network.

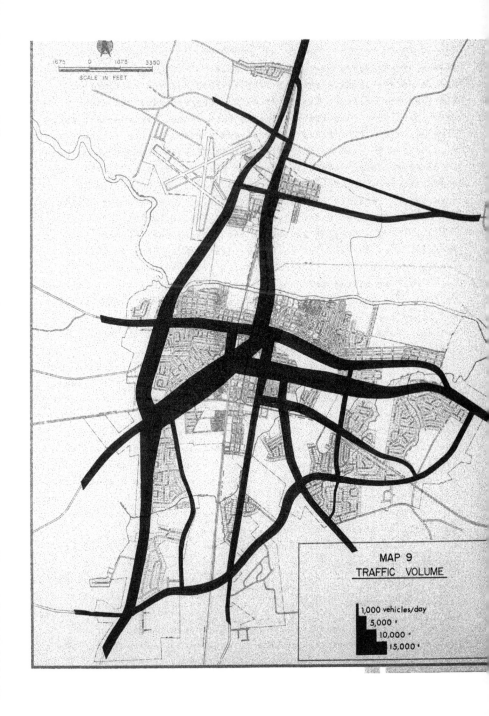

SCALE IN FEET

1675   0   1675   3350

MAP 9
TRAFFIC VOLUME

1,000 vehicles/day
5,000 "
10,000 "
15,000 "

Greenville's present thoroughfare plan tends to promote further growth in the general directions where the cities
services are already over extended - toward the south and the
southeast, whereas no attempt is evident in promoting development,
residential or industrial, in areas that may eventually give a
resemblance of balance of physical growth. The areas are those
in the direction of west, southwest and some parts in the north.
A revised traffic system should take proper corrective actions
regarding the above stated deficiencies.

II. The Specifics - Streets, Intersections, Crossings
and Others. The overall quality of a thoroughfare is to be determined by a combination of many factors. Among these various
factors, however, traffic carrying capacity during the peak traffic
hours and traffic safety loom as the two more significant determinants and are usually assigned heavier weight during the course
of assessment. In Map 8, the relative quality of several heavily
used urban arterials in Greenville is portrayed through the visual
device of "travel time contour combined with pinpointed accident
locations involving motor vehicles." The contour data was gathered
in several consecutive weekdays of July 1965 and represent the
average results of four runs conducted during afternoon rush hours
between 4:00 to 5:30 p.m. The contours are plotted along 30 second time intervals at speeds not exceeding those permitted within
the districts. The information related to traffic accidents covers
a period from January to May of 1966 and is provided by the Greenville Police Department.

By cross-referencing with Map 9 which shows the traffic volumes of major thoroughfares, the graphics of Map 8 reveal
several interesting points about the local traffic conditions.
First, only one arterial, South Evans Street, is judged both safe
and adequate in handling rush hour traffic in serving the growing
southern sectors of the community. This fact is illustrated by
the bulge formed by the contours along the thoroughfares in con-
trast to the deep valleys which represent a relative lack of progress in the distance traveled during the same time interval.

West Fifth Street is not as adequate as Evans Street, but it carries a considerable larger volume of traffic until Memorial Drive is reached. Beyond that intersection, very limited numbers of motoring public are being served by this arterial.

The pace of vehicular progress along either Charles Street or Fourteenth is less than that of South Evans Street. This may well be attributed to the existence of several right angle turns along the alignments. It should be noted that during some Saturday afternoons, the combined traffic generated by Pitt Plaza and Ficklen Stadium would put a considerable "dent" on the contours along Charles Street.

East Fifth Street, handicapped by numerous entrances into the College and carrying considerable amounts of traffic, has proved to be a surprisingly good carrier of peak hour traffic. Undoubtedly, adjacent Fourth Street certainly has been a help in siphoning off an unknown but sizable volume of traffic. The relatively high performance of East Fifth Street is achieved, however, at the expense of traffic safety. Accident corners abound along this route.

The inadequacy of North Green Street and the bridge are dramatically illustrated in the "travel time contour" map. First, the traffic volume along the route just to the north of the bridge is the second highest recorded anywhere within the planning area.* This high volume of traffic, compounded by the large number of turning movements south of the river is forced through an antiquated two-lane bridge. The congestion resulting may be better illustrated by the following test: If two motorists are heading home during the rush hour from Five Points, before the northbound commuter can cross the river, the westbound motorist would have reached a point some quarter mile west of the Memorial Hospital. The urgent need to improve the present situation along this radial cannot be overstressed.

---

*1964 Average Annual Daily Traffic Figure: 7,600 vehicles.

- 35 -

Considering the high traffic volume as well as a
large number of turning movements along the route, Dickinson
Avenue is actually a much better urban arterial than generally
recognized. To be sure, the motorist can make only half the
mileage along Dickinson if he were to travel along South Evans
Street for the same elapsed time.

But, again, the highest traffic volume recorded anywhere within the community occurs at Dickinson Avenue between the
railroad overpass and West End Circle.* A series of traffic
bottlenecks occur in this vicinity: first, the high traffic volume
along Dickinson Avenue, hemmed in by the railroad tracks crossing
overhead at an acute angle, complicated further by the intrusion
of Hooker Road and then the presence of the poor intersection at
West End Circle may well be the chief contributing cause that prevents any significant extent of urban development west of the
Memorial Drive-South Dickinson axis.

The most dramatic revelation of all by the travel time
contour map is the glaring inadequacy of Tenth Street as a thoroughfare. This is the street with the undesirable conditions of high
traffic volume,** high turning movement, high pedestrian traffic
crossing, narrow two travel lanes with parking permitted on both
sides, not to speak of the driving characteristics of the student
drivers and the mounting pressures to develop the roadside pro-
perties in strip commercial fashion. All these converge and pro-
duce a predicament that is rapidly approaching the crisis point as
far as traffic situations are concerned. Prompt remedial steps
need to be taken on an emergency basis as well as preventive steps
backed up by a sound land use versus traffic policy which requires
the utmost in cooperation of the municipality, highway, and college
officials.

---

*1964 A.A.D.T. figure: 11,500 vehicles.
**1964 A.A.D.T. figure: 7,200 vehicles.

There exists an uncommonly large number of substandard intersections. The more important ones are listed below, along with the nature of their deficiencies. These are deemed important by virtue of their more strategic locations in relation to the overall traffic network of the city. These selections do not coincide with those pointed out in the Traffic Hazard Survey conducted by the Greenville Junior Chamber of Commerce in early 1966. The explanation for this discrepancy is that the Jaycees' attention has been focused more on the specific neighborhood level whereas those listed below have significantly greater impact on the thoroughfare system as a whole.

a. Memorial Drive and Bethel Highway at Greenfield Terrace acute angle intersection.

b. Pactolus Highway (N.C. 30) and Belvoir Road at Bethel Highway - jog along a high speed thoroughfare.

c. West End Circle - high traffic volume, bad north-south alignment along Memorial Drive and South Dickinson Avenue.

d. South Dickinson and Greenville Boulevard - acute angle intersection.

e. South Evans Street and Greenville Boulevard - acute angle intersection.

f. Charles Street (N.C. 43) and Greenville Boulevard - potential five point intersection according to current proposal.

g. Fourteenth Street and Greenville Boulevard - five point intersection.

h. East Fifth and East Tenth Streets at Colonial Height - acute angle intersection.

i. Cotanche and Charles Street at Tenth Street - jog along an otherwise through arterial.

j. Five Points in downtown - dangerous five point intersection.

k. West Fifth Street at Albemarle Street - jog along a through arterial.

l. Tenth Street and Dickinson Avenue at A.C.L. railroad tracks - chaotic intersection with high traffic volumes and turning movements compounded by freight trains crossing at grade.

m. Charles Street at Norfolk and Southern tracks - subject to flooding by overflow from Green Mill Run at the underpass.

n. South Evans Street at Green Mill Run - subject to flooding.

o. Hooker Road at Green Mill Run - same as above.

p. East Tenth Street at Green Mill Run - same as above.

q. East Fifth Street at Green Mill Run - same as above.

r. Greenville Boulevard at Fornes Run - same as above.

s. Dickinson Avenue at Norfolk and Southern underpass - subject to flooding.

t. Mumford Road and Pactolus Highway (not in City - acute angle intersection complicated by a newly paved road which leads to mobile home park at intersection.

III. Policy. Except for a section* on the dedications of right-of-way for boulevards and thoroughfares and the aforementioned thoroughfare plan in the City Code, there is no other official municipal policy declared concerning the community's long range traffic needs.** East Carolina College, the largest traffic generator within the city by far, has not made known to the public its policies regarding parking and traffic in general - if any such policies exist. The North Carolina State Highway Commission is entrusted with the duty of reviewing the layouts of new constructions along those thoroughfares included in the State system. So far, with the noted exceptions of roads designated as limited access and controlled access, none of which are in existence locally, the reviewing power has proved to be singularly unsuccessful in controlling roadside strip commercial developments (a subject discussed in a previous section) or in dealing with the growth of the campus such as the traffic exigencies along Tenth Street as previously mentioned. In short, much is to be desired at the policy making level for all three public agencies, as far as traffic planning within this community is concerned.

It is not within the scope of this study to evaluate the policies of either the Highway Commission or the College. However, their cooperation is indispensable in solving the existing traffic problems as well as in helping the community in attaining the goals which are duly spelled forth in the coming chapter.

---

* Greenville City Code, Appendix B, Section 4.
** Parking regulations are not included as basic policies.

The City of Greenville can achieve a great deal by
itself in dealing with the traffic problems present or anticipated. By controlling the density of development along the major
arterials, traffic friction can be considerably reduced. This
may be done through the provisions of a revised zoning ordinance
which may also legally prescribe the nature of land use along the
major roadways. By revising the current thoroughfare plan, the
rather perverted pattern of overgrowth may become more balanced
and some of the worst traffic bottlenecks currently in existence
may be remedied and at the same time prevent the formation of new
ones. By taking certain steps to alter the traffic pattern around
the College and in the central business district, more cars can
drive through existing streets to the greater safety of both
motorists and pedestrians.

CHAPTER III - THE PLAN AND ITS IMPLEMENTATION

Section 1. Community Goals and Planning Objectives

Greenville has been making news headlines of late. It is apparent that there are now and will be even more activities which will emanate from this city. The community leaders are working hard toward achieving certain objectives for Greenville. Such a desired state of affairs forms the basis of community goals, the more specific of which, such as those which concern the land development, are termed planning objectives.

The realization of the community goals through the implementation of planning objectives must eventually take place within the physical confines of the community. A better Greenville tomorrow is to be superimposed over the Greenville of today. For this reason, the foregoing sections in the previous chapter have been devoted to the analysis of the existing development within the planning area.

What are the professed community goals of Greenville that local leaders are striving to achieve? Listed below without priority are some of the more significant ones:

- Greenville is to become not only the higher educational center but also the cultural and entertainment center of the Coastal Plain Region of North Carolina through the logical expansion and extension of current facilities of East Carolina College.

- Greenville is to expand substantially its industrial employment opportunities through the provision of potential plant sites, the extension of utilities and the accessibility of a sound transportation network that includes highway, railroad and air.

- Greenville is to solidify its position as the shopping center of the region by upgrading the existing centrally located facilities through the process of urban renewal and also by expanding new shopping facilities by providing greater vehicular accessibility and parking ease.

- Greenville is to become, education as well as facility wise, the medical center of the Coastal Plain Region of the State through the effort of and the cooperation by both the college and the general public.

- Greenville is to maintain its leading position as a tobacco marketing center in the State by expanding and modernizing the existing warehousing facilities.

- Greenville is to set itself as an exemplar community of the growing east by upgrading the overall level of livability through the improvement of various community facilities and traffic conditions.

The above listed are by no means an exhaustive list of goals commonly accepted by the community. These six statements merely represent the most central ones of the current local issues concerning the community growth. The planning objectives prescribed in the subsequent sections are all based on the above stated community wide aspirations.

Section 2. Particular Planning Considerations

In the course of formulating the planning objectives for the community based upon the previously stated broad community goals, several local planning considerations were consistently noticed. Disregarding these considerations would necessarily result in a land development plan that is based upon a false, or at best, a noncomprehensive premise. Such a plan could not be counted on to carry out goals and objectives of the community. It is deemed proper, therefore, to give air to these considerations.

I. The Changing Role of Downtown Greenville. As the suburbia grows, the position of the downtown is relatively weakened. Without doubt, the growth of the suburbs is achieved at the expense of the core of the community. This has already happened in Greenville, as has happened almost everywhere else throughout the country.

The decentralization of activities that formerly belonged to downtown is all but an irreversible process. Very few enterprises that have migrated outward have been known to be tempted back. Lack of capable communication and transportation systems decrees a close in location for many businesses. The rising number of car owners, the improvement in highway facilities and an ample supply of vacant land, all combine to make shabby contrasts of the downtown business precinct where high rent, scarce and inconvenient parking, obsolete physical plants, difficulty in land assemblage plus a host of other blighting factors prevail.

The pace of this nearly irreversible process may be greatly decelerated or even completely halted for a certain length of time by the process of urban renewal, two projects of which are in varied state of progress in Greenville. One must not, however, entertain such false hope that downtown Greenville, through the magical attributes of urban renewal, will soon once again capture the market lost to the satellite commercial centers. The old adage about the fundamental strategy of "arriving there firstest with the mostest" certainly applies in this situation. One should not overlook the fact that there can be only so many consumer dollars to be spent in and to be shared by the downtown and the outlying stores.

The weakened position of downtown Greenville may in the future be bolstered, however, through the urban renewal process in the following ways.

- To prevent the further erosion of the downtown retail potential, restrictions through the provisions of a properly revised zoning ordinance be placed on the establishment of new shopping centers.

- To emphasize and foster the growth of certain existing functions within the downtown area, governmental administrative agencies, professional and institutional offices and those similar types of activities that emphasize face-to-face contacts and an exchange of information rather than bulky goods should be properly encouraged, again through the provisions of a revised zoning ordinance.

- To make downtown Greenville the neighborhood convenience shopping and activity center for the thousands of students and faculty residing nearby. This functional affinity is reinforced by their proximity. But in order for such a functional relation to work properly over a long period of time, the large volume of pedestrian traffic traveling between the campus and the downtown must not be interrupted by fast moving vehicular traffic to any significant extent.

II. Industrialization without Urbanization. Another significant phenomenon observed within the Coastal Plain Region is that the industrialization in or near a community does not spur a proportional residential growth within the community itself.* This appears to be a unique Eastern Carolina phenomena. Depending upon such variables as average regional income and educational levels, it is found that an increase in average pay brings about a proportional larger number of workers commuting from a greater distance. This particular condition has been locally confirmed.** Only one out of three industrial workers employed in Greenville actually resides within the city. Such findings may, in a fashion, act as guides to seek the locational determinants for industrial land uses in the future. The higher paying industrial plants seem to be locationally more suited for the outlying addresses situated on or near highways that ensure easier accessibility for the long distance commuters. A higher parking ratio should be applied in the estimation of parking spaces in recognition of the fact that the workers must arrive at work by cars. Thus, it seems that almost by default, the comparatively lower paying industrial concerns may take the more inlying industrial sites in order to be more centrally situated for the workers who live in the city.

    III. Constraints Due to the Capacities of Utility Systems and Soil Conditions. For most growing communities, the capacity of the municipal utility systems: water, sewer, etc., normally constitutes a major constraint for future development. The extension of these public works together with that of streets are the prime determinants for the physical growth of a neighborhood providing the land to be developed fulfills certain preconditions such as size, topographical and soil conditions.

---

    *See "Some Implications of Long Distance Commuting in North Carolina", unpublished paper by R. E. Longsdale, Geography Department, U.N.C., Chapel Hill, N. C., February, 1966.

    **See Population and Economy of Greenville, N. C., Division of Community Planning, 1965.

As a result of Greenville's persistent quest for a
eater share of regional industrial growth during the recent years,
e capacities of various individual utility systems* are more than
equate for any immediate residential or commercial growth – either
which places much lighter demand upon the systems than industrial
owth would. Thus strictly from the land use planning standpoint,
e respective capacities of each branch of the utility system does
t constitute a significant constraint to any future growth taking
ace within the planning area.

The role of the geography of the land, however, comes
to play concerning the future extension policy of sewage trunk
nes. To the south of the river, the urban development in the
rections from south (N.C. 11) to east (U.S. 264) is rapidly
proaching the ridge line of the drainage basin of the system
ich entirely gravity flow in mode of operation south of the river.
nce, any further development to the south or southeast of
lvedere, Lynndale, Oakmont and Eastwood, would require a lift
ation – an expensive proposition. Since the operation of the
ty's utility system is a revenue producing or at least self
staining one, while the other municipal services are by and large
ney losing ones, it is reasonable to suggest that, for all future
tensions beyond the ridge line, a detailed cost and benefit
alysis should be made in order to determine the feasibility of
y such requests.

Topographical features within the planning area are
ch that none of them constitutes a deterrent to physical growth
ywhere in the community. There are no extreme geological features
ch as sharp grade (over nine percent in grade), escarpment or
ammoth outcropping of rock formations, or cliffs other than those
ound in a mild form along the south bank of the Tar River. It
ay be regrettable that most of the terrain variations – unusual

---

*The capacity of the municipal sewage system is recently
rther bolstered by $330,000 federal matching grant for the con-
truction of a new sewer outfall system in North Greenville for
erving the emerging industrial complex in that area.

for the Coastal Plain Region - are not used to advantage in an architectural sense during the development. But a critique of this nature does not belong to the scope of this study.

Soil condition is no deterrent to growth within the areas that are served by the city utility systems, with two exceptions: nine types of soil are located within the planning area. These are: Caroline Series (Ns1), Lakeland Sand (LS), Portsmouth Rains and Lynchberg (P1), Coxville Silt Loam (C), Swamp (S) and Muck (M). Of the nine, only the last two - swamp and muck - are not conducive for higher development anywhere within the planning area, whether served by the municipal system or not. Swampy soil contains a mixture of alluvial material found along the lowlying, periodically inundated area such as the broad belt of lowland just north of the river and along its tributaries: Green Mill and Fornes Runs. This type of soil is characterized by a high content of organic material; hence the bearing strength is very poor. Its very location identifies itself with that of the very poorly drained terrain subjected to overflow of nearby streams or river. From the aerial photos, this class of soil stands out easily as a darkened belt of vegetation growth.

Similar in characteristics is muck, which is found in various pockets to the northwest of the urbanized area, mainly along the banks of the Tar River. This type of soil is much less extensive in distribution as compared to swamp.

Some of these lowlying tracts are priced high due to their locational advantages. To the unwary buyer, any higher form of urban development may well prove to be a costly misventure. This is due to the poorly drained lowlying terrain as much as to the nature of the soil itself.

Section 3. Land Development Plan

The text in this section serves as the verbal counterpart of the graphics shown in Map 10, the Land Development Plan. Through the medium of the graphics, the stated planning objectives for the community thus take a more concrete form. On the map, the functional arrangement of major categories of land uses and the

- 45 -

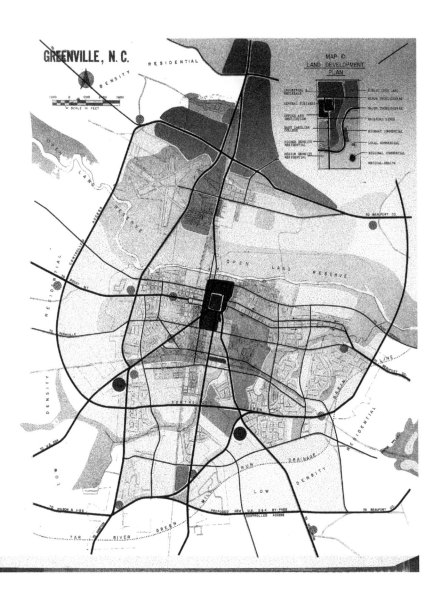

GREENVILLE, N. C.

RESIDENTIAL

MAP 10
LAND DEVELOPMENT
PLAN

superimposed traffic network are shown together. The traffic
network pattern represents the revised version of the existing
thoroughfare plan.

Together, the graphics and the text are intended to
show, from the vantage point of today, the most rational way in
which Greenville may be physically developed, given broad community
goals and objectives. The Plan should not be construed, therefore,
as the ultimate plan of the community for all times. Enumerated
below are the planning objectives that highlight the physical
plan.

I. The Accommodation of the Growth of East Carolina
College. As the college enrollment continues to rise, the need
for more facilities increases accordingly. It is estimated, at
present, that the enrollment may reach 12,000 students before
1980 is reached. The expansion of physical plants in order to
keep pace with this increase makes enlargement of the present
campus mandatory. In preparation to meet future requirements of
the college, the following measures concerning land use in and
around the campus are properly reflected in the Land Development
Plan.

    a. Increased land utilization by spacing future
       buildings closer together and between existing
       buildings and facilities.

    b. Acquisition of more land area adjacent to the
       original campus near the center of Greenville.

    c. Eventual development of a traffic control system
       that would allow motor vehicle access to all
       campus areas but no through motor vehicle traffic.

    d. Establishment of vehicle parking areas in strategic
       locations mainly on the fringe of the campus.

    e. Establishment of a pedestrain overpass(es) across
       Tenth Street thus connecting the north and middle
       campus. Bicycles should be able to cross over
       although motor scooters and motorcycles should be
       prohibited.

II. The Compaction of the Residential Districts
Surrounding the College Campus. Higher residential density is to
become a reality in the neighborhoods immediately surrounding the
college. Increasingly larger numbers of students and college

- 46 -

personnel may then walk to places of activities thus lessening
the traffic congestion which may otherwise result. The desired
higher residential density should not be construed as a license
for overcrowding, a major cause for urban blight. This means a
more efficient use of close in urban land. Usable outdoor living
and recreation spaces are not to sacrificed. (See planning
objectives on recreation needs below).

III. The Fruitful Effort of Urban Renewal — A New
Central Business District. The elimination of Five Points means
the elimination of much traffic congestion and hazard. New
physical plants for retail, commercial, and professional uses
south of Fifth Street on either side of Evans Street add new life
to the downtown precinct. To the north, west and south of the
renewed retail core is to be a semicircular ring of professional
type of offices, financial and governmental institutions, interspersed by the supporting convenience trade facilities such as
fine restaurants, coffee houses, theatres, barber shops, beauty
parlors and other such establishments that add variety to a
thriving downtown. The bulk of new off-street parking spaces are
to be located to the north, west and south of the retail core.

More parking emphasis is provided on the west of
downtown since it runs parallel to the axis of the retail core.
It may be seen that heavy vehicular traffic is purposely excluded
from the east edge of the central business district. It is deemed
very unwise to drive a motorized wedge between the college and
retail and convenience service core of the renewed downtown. The
very heavy pedestrian traffic created between the two activities is
given a guaranteed right-of-way. Should a north-south oriented
thoroughfare to the east of downtown become absolutely necessary,
the natural gulley or depression which now exists (part of it is
used as a school playground) may be utilized as the right-of-way
of a depressed parkway that will cross under all the east-west
oriented streets from Second to Fifth Streets. This parkway may
terminate at First Street where a marina adjacent to a landscaped
town common is currently being proposed by the local Redevelopment
Commission.

Filling in the Nonurban Tracts. The many currently
vacant tracts south of the Tar River bypassed by the leapfrogging
surburban growth are proposed to be filled in with medium or higher
density type of residential development. It is estimated that at
an average density of 3.0 dwelling units per gross acre, up to
2,100 new dwelling units or some 7,000 new residents can be
accommodated in over 1,100 acres of prime developable land. This
figure represents almost 30 percent of all existing dwelling units
within the city. Thus by filling in the webs between the fingers
of growth and by the compaction of the more inlying residential
neighborhoods, the population of Greenville may be substantially
increased, by as much as perhaps 10,000 people, without further
enlarging the outer limits of the current development.

Developing Outlying Residential Areas that are Within
the Current Capability of the Municipal Utility Systems. The
considerable amount of acreage situated to the west of N.C. 11
(Memorial Drive and South Dickinson Avenue) are within the drainage
basin of the city's gravity flow sewerage system. Location wise,
the bulk of these vacant or farmlands are certainly no further
from downtown facilities or the emerging industrial centers in
north Greenville than Fairland or Lakewood Pines. Priority for
development of these outlying areas is not as high as the two
previous stated objectives, although it is rated ahead of those
areas lying beyond the ridgeline of local drainage system.

The Accommodation of Better Recreational Facilities
Through the Expansion of More Recreational Land. More than twice
the current acreage for recreational purpose is needed to serve
even the present population. These additional acres, properly
located in different neighborhoods for various recreational
purposes: tot lots, neighborhood parks and playground, nonurban
parks, etc., are absolute requisites for the accommodation of the
physical facilities to be installed. Generally they are distributed
in the Plan according to the anticipated neighborhood density as
well as the current deficits of such land. Land bordering along
the banks of the Tar River and its tributaries is judged unsuited

for higher urban uses, although these marginal lands may be banded together in long stretches to form a series of finger like green-belts.

Reconstitution of the Inlying Industrial Neighborhoods. The declining inlying industrial neighborhoods bordering on rail-road trunk lines and spurs deep within the community are to be given a new lease on life. New alignment of urban arterials and greater ease of land assemblage, both achievable through the process of urban renewal, are the principal means to bring out the realization of an intown industrial park.

Preservation of Prime Land in the Outlying Districts For Industrial Purposes. In north Greenville, currently available large acreage of nonurban land in the close vicinity of a combin-ation of noncongested highways, railroads and spur lines, airport service while readily served by the community's utility systems are held in reserve for the expected arrival of new industries.

Formation of Medical Health Complex in Western Suburbs of Greenville. Ready vehicular access, availability of suitable land, budding medical facilities already in existence plus the community desire for more locally based health related facilities combined to give impetus to the creation of such a complex in the western edge of the community. The formation of this complex would make Greenville the center of one more urban function of the region.

Completion of Circumferential Loop Connecting Both Sides of Tar River. From what is the current eastern terminal of U. S. 264 Bypass, the proposed alignment crosses the River, proceeds northward in a counterclockwise fashion and intersects with Pactolus Highway (N. C. 30) until the Bethel Highway (N. C. 11) is reached in the vicinity of the Dail Farm. The above forms the eastern link of the circumferential loop. Proceeding westward from a point just north of Pitt Plaza following the proposed alignment of N. C. 43 Bypass till South Dickinson Avenue is reached, intersecting with U. S. 264, Stantonsburg Road, and Falkland Highway (N. C. 43) crossing the river and merging with Belvoir Highway until the Bethel Highway is again reached.

The completion of the loop will do much not only to expedite traffic between the emerging industrial center in the north and the residential sections of the city south of the River, but also to serve as a major instrument to develop the prime virgin land to the west and to the north of the city for the reasons stated previously. Among various portions of the circumferential loop, the southwest quadrant from Falkland Highway to Pitt Plaza is rated as top priority and the northeast quadrant from U. S. 264 east to the Bethel Highway is almost as urgent. It should be pointed out that the proposed alignment of the loop also serves to enhance the locational advantage of the proposed medical health complex as well by being more accessible from almost anywhere within the county region.

More Elaborate Technical Solutions Warranted at Two Major Intersections. Two intersections which may soon become the two worst traffic bottlenecks in the eastern part of the State need timely treatment in order to avert such predicaments. The intersection at West End Circle, complicated by the railroad overpass nearby and the proposed Five Point intersection at Pitt Plaza, need more than the routine array of traffic signals and islands to handle adequately the peak hour traffic. In order to keep the traffic flowing during such periods without relying upon regiments of local and state policemen to direct traffic, some kind of traffic interchanges or grade separations appear to be the only recourse. This would eliminate, at least to a certain extent, the main stream of heavy traffic crossing at the grade. The more detailed layouts for these two intersections are beyond the scope of this study. In the plan, it is deemed sufficient to just indicate their proposed locations.

Pedestrian Crossings or Plaza Partially Crossing Over Tenth Street. The worsening conditions relating to the traffic flow and pedestrian safety between the north and middle campus of the College do not at the present time leave too many alternatives for solutions. Several pedestrian crossings over Tenth Street could be one type of solution, or a landscaped pedestrian plaza interconnecting the two campuses may be the other solution. The first alternative is by far more expedient whereas the second alternative has architectural merits that are more befitting to both the College and the City, but at a much larger cost. The stretch of Tenth Street in question, it may be noted, is not topographically unsuited for such a suggestion as the street enters the vicinity in a gentle downward grade from the west.

One-Way Coupling of Fourth and Fifth Streets. High volume of both local and through traffic and the high incidence of traffic accidents on Fourth and Fifth Streets prompts the proposal of one-way coupling of these two streets. Widening of either street necessarily involves extreme measures: chopping down a sizable number of old trees along Fifth Street and reducing the already minimal front yard setbacks along Fourth Street. Traffic safety can be significantly improved by the one-way coupling. But the main virtue of such a device is to improve the carrying capacity of both streets. For a typical urban street in the uptown district with a 40 foot pavement width and with parking permitted on one side, the street capacity* is about 1,250 vehicles per hour two-way. The capacity is increased to 2,786 vehicles per hour if one-way traffic is adopted. Even allowing parking on both sides of a one-way street, the capacity remains 50 percent higher at 1,880 vehicles per hour. Therefore, for reasons of carrying capacity, traffic safety as well as possible more on-street parking,** the one-way coupling is an urgent must. The question remains as to where the one-way pattern should begin. East of Elm Street, traffic volume drops off by over 50 percent, so that no great need to continue the suggested pattern exists east of Elm. But there is no place west of that intersection where a diagonal street can cut through without the physical removal of a large number of dwellings. It is necessary, therefore, from the economics standpoint, to have such a diagonal occur at either of the two locations shown in the Plan — east of Hilltop Street or east of Beech Street.

---

*See Highway Capacity Manual, U. S. Bureau of Public Roads, Washington, D. C., 1950

**This measure is not being endorsed in this study.

<u>New Traffic Flow Pattern for Renewed Downtown</u>
<u>Greenville.</u> It has been mentioned previously in this section
that the general intent of the revised downtown traffic pattern
is to let the traffic as well as the bulk of off-street parking
ring around the three sides of the pedestrian oriented downtown
retail core – to the north, west and south – so that the future
downtown can be physically tied more closely to the College
nearby. The through traffic in the east-west direction must now
rely upon a new thoroughfare linking the Greene-Pitt one-way
couple to Cotanche Street. This street may be located just to
the north of Seventh Street. There is also the possibility of
utilizing the natural gulley which exists between the college
and downtown as a future grade separated parkway. The merits
of this proposal should be given a more detailed study.

      <u>Reservation of New Corridor For Bypassing the Bypass.</u>
Not being a limited access or even a controlled access street
with paralleling service street, Greenville Boulevard (U. S. 264
Bypass) will soon become a highly congested local thoroughfare
with literally thousands of curb cuts and driveway entrances.*
The fast developing areas to the east, such as Beaufort County,
will also draw a sizable volume of truck traffic as well as an
expectedly large number of cars towing boats and trailers through
the southern suburbs of Greenville. Such almost inevitable predicaments concerning the use of the present bypass warrants the
timely setting aside of a corridor that may in time serve as the
new alignment of the relocated U. S. 264 Bypass. That the new
bypass should be strictly limited access in character needs no
further elaboration. The alignment proposed is considerably to
the south of existing urbanized areas. It is proposed to inter-
sect N. C. 43 at a point some one and one-half miles southeast
of Pitt Plaza, and to proceed counterclockwise in a broad curve
passing near Brook Valley from the southeast and rejoin the

_____

    *See the analysis of the existing situation in Section 3,
Chapter 2 of this Study.

existing U. S. 264 just to the west of the community of Simpson. This proposed corridor is designed to utilize the existing county road rights-of-way to the fullest extent permissible.

Section 4. Suggested Steps In Implementing The Plan

Lest the objectives set forth in the previous pages become mere empty words and lay dormant hereafter in the archives, concrete steps must be taken and actions must be initiated in order to insure the timely realization of these community dreams. The public and private sectors alike share the civic burden of the implementation of the prepared plan. It should be made clear to all that the purpose is not to implement the plan for its own sake, but by going through the process of implementation, the long sought, hard fought goals of the community may stand a better chance of becoming a reality.

It may be duly noted that not all of the planning objectives share equal exigency. Some are necessarily longer range in nature than others. There are, nevertheless, certain steps related to the field of community planning that must be first taken before the other planning objectives can be properly carried out. These requisites are listed below, not, however, in the order of priority.

I. Establishment of Municipal Planning Framework. Within the municipal administrative framework, the long needed position of City Planner should be created and filled. Such a position demands the qualification of a full-time, technically trained professional planner, supported with a staff of adequate size. Administratively responsible to the city manager, the planner shall address himself to the following tasks:

- To conduct needed studies related to community planning matters and to offer alternative solutions to the problems identified.

- To formulate, amend and interpret the plans, regulations, ordinances and programs related to planning for the city.

- To coordinate various physical development projects that are taking place within the community and to synchronize the goals and objectives of these various projects.

- To report to the City Planning and Zoning Commission on all planning issues on the current agenda.
- To answer the inquiring public on questions pertaining to planning matters.
- To provide physical planning aid to other municipal and other governmental agencies.

II. A Revised Zoning Ordinance*. An extensive revision of the existing ordinance is now being effected at the planning board level. Its basic framework as well as its regulatory provisions are being updated. The ordinance will be modified to better fit the needs of the community. Flexibility will be introduced by the inclusion of the provisions for conditional uses in addition to permitted uses. This inclusion will do much in shedding the straight jacketing influence of a too rigid ordinance. The revised ordinance will be cognizant of the land use objectives set forth in this study for it is through the proper administering of the revised zoning ordinance that the bulk of the basic planning objectives contained herein will be implemented.

III. A Revised Thoroughfare Plan. The function of a traffic network is not only to serve the existing development but to promote desired future growth as well. The revised plan should properly reflect the basic objectives set forth in the Land Development Plan in which the revised thoroughfare alignments are suggested.

The urgency of the planning proposals contained therein varies considerably and a priority system shall be established. Some of the proposed objectives may be achieved through the process of urban renewal (See suggestion V below) while others may be gained by cooperative efforts involving both the municipality and North Carolina State Highway Commission.

_____

*The revision of the existing ordinance is currently underway by the Planning Board with the technical assistance of the Division of Community Planning.

IV. Closer Working Liason With East Carolina College.
The expectant growth of the College in the near future cannot be
properly accommodated by the community at large without a closer
working relationship than that has heretofore existed. During
the next several years, such vexing problems as parking, traffic
patterns, further expansion of campus facilities, and other college
related planning issues demand an intensified dialogue between the
town and the gown. There should be a formal channel established
so that the municipality, the college and the planning consultants
retained by each may have ready and frequent consultations.

V. Synchronization of Planning Goals and Objectives
With the Local Urban Renewal and Housing Authority. The process
of urban renewal is in fact the most expeditious means to implement
the planning objectives delineated in the Land Development Plan.
In no way is this very thorough and costly a process meant to be
an end unto itself, in separate pursuit of objectives that are
independent from that of the community as a comprehensive whole.
The need to compare and to synchronize the basic planning objectives in terms of land use, housing need and traffic pattern is,
therefore, a basic one. Periodic consultation among the planning
personnel of various governmental agencies in order to facilitate
such a synchronization should be required.

VI. Consultation with Other Public Agencies Concerning
the Physical Development of the Community. In spurring urbanization of an area, there exist other major development tools in
addition to the extension of the street system. These equally
important determinants for promoting growth include the extension
of the utility systems, the placement of new schools, libraries
and other neighborhood serving public facilities. The policies
governing the future expansion of these systems and facilities
shall be made consonant with that of the municipality as a whole.
At present, consultation and alignment of basic planning goals
among public agencies whose operations significantly affect the
future growth pattern of the community does not exist. This
situation should be amended as soon as possible.

VII. **Advance Land Acquisition in Anticipation of**
Future Municipal Use. Investment in real estate usually guarantees
a handsome financial return over a period of years. This fact
explains, in an oblique way, the need for the municipality to
acquire or otherwise gain control of the needed acreage now for
various anticipated municipal uses in the future. What is not
soon purchased will certainly be doubled or tripled in price when
needs arise in the future. A myriad of federal and state financial
aid programs are already in existence that could be applied to a
variety of municipal purposes: parks and recreational land,
schools, reservoirs, water sheds, sanitary land fills and many
others. These possibilities should be looked into and the detailed future land use needs should be ascertained accordingly.

VIII. **Exploration and Determination of Real Local**
Housing Needs. Physical deterioration of housing structures is
far from being the only cause of residential blight. There are
other more subtle and more pervasive incongruous factors at work
that undermine the general livability of this community. Various
forms of private inconveniences and rising public costs together
make any given community a less desirable place to live in the
long run. Public housing merely erases the physical symptoms of
a limited number of local poor. The plight of the other higher
income groups being regarded as less exigent is often left un-
attended. It has been known for sometime that the prevailing
phenomenon of the postwar suburbanization featuring single
detached dwellings on ten thousand square foot lots provides true
comfort to only a few while increasing higher hidden cost, social
or financial, to nearly all. The emerging white-collared community
of Greenville should examine its real housing needs suited for
the local residents and take appropriate steps in fulfilling them.
Previously stated planning objectives deal with this problem only
in the broadest fashion — a halt to further suburban sprawl in
conjunction with inner compaction as the preliminary steps. Needed to be looked into in greater details are such federal financially
aided so-called 221d3 housing programs* that aim to benefit middle

---

*Refer to Neighborhood Analysis, Greenville, N. C.

income families by providing housing at low or no profit margins. Provision of housing of these types more often than not is accompanied by a reduction of waste in land use as compaction without congestion is inherent with such building programs.

IX. Innovations in Subdivision Practice. As a corollary to the above suggestion, there are current innovations in subdivision practice that are designed to enhance the amenity of the neighborhood without the usual increase of either private or public cost. Cluster housing and group development types of subdivisions are two among many. In either type mentioned above, usable outdoor space is increased and greater architectural design possibility permitted without introducing higher costs to any sector of the community. The overall density of the neighborhood is maintained while the yard dimensions* are being adjusted to optimal sizes. The publicly acclaimed new communities such as Reston and Columbia in Maryland use such innovations liberally. For the proper functioning of these practices the plans should be prepared by technically competent architects and reviewed by an equally competent planning staff of the city. This suggestion is urged because the libability character of Greenville in the future depends to a great extent upon the acceptance of these innovations.

X. Further Planning Studies Required. This study is purported to provide planning information at a general level. The specifics of various elements should be detailed in a series of further studies. Evaluations and plans for the various municipal facilities serving the current and anticipated community needs can be incorporated in a future study, the Community Facilities Plan. The programing of the needs for these facilities as well as the individual amount of cost and sources of revenue can be included in a Public Improvements Program and Capital Improvements Budget. The explosive growth that has occurred within the planning area during the recent years has nearly ruined the community's

---

*In most cases, the rear and side yards are adjusted.

once charming appearance. A back log of beauty treatment problems
which are more than skin deep can be comprehensively discussed in
depth in a <u>Community Appearance Study</u>. The ever outward extending
limbs of the city thoroughfares have created numerous transportation
problems, some of which are unique to Greenville. The feasibility
of creating a mass transportation network deserves timely consideration. A study may properly be addressed to this increasingly
important matter.

      As has been pointed out previously, this report should
not at all be construed as <u>the</u> plan for the community for all
times. New events and new outlooks demand periodic re-examination
of community goals as well as the previously formulated plans.